TEACHER'S PET PUBLICATIONS

LITPLAN TEACHER PACK
for
Sounder
based on the book by
William Armstrong

Written by
Mary B. Collins

© 1996 Teacher's Pet Publications
All Rights Reserved

This **LitPlan** for William Armstrong's
Sounder
has been brought to you by Teacher's Pet Publications, Inc.

Copyright Teacher's Pet Publications 1996
11504 Hammock Point
Berlin MD 21811

Only the student materials in this unit plan (such as worksheets,
study questions, and tests) may be reproduced multiple times
for use in the purchaser's classroom.

For any additional copyright questions,
contact Teacher's Pet Publications.

www.tpet.com

TABLE OF CONTENTS - *Sounder*

Introduction	5
Unit Objectives	7
Reading Assignment Sheet	8
Unit Outline	9
Study Questions (Short Answer)	13
Quiz/Study Questions (Multiple Choice)	18
Pre-reading Vocabulary Worksheets	31
Lesson One (Introductory Lesson)	43
Nonfiction Assignment Sheet	46
Oral Reading Evaluation Form	48
Writing Assignment 1	45
Writing Assignment 2	50
Writing Assignment 3	58
Writing Evaluation Form	59
Vocabulary Review Activities	53
Extra Writing Assignments/Discussion ?s	54
Unit Review Activities	60
Unit Tests	63
Unit Resource Materials	91
Vocabulary Resource Materials	107

A FEW NOTES ABOUT THE AUTHOR
William Armstrong

William Armstrong was born on September 14, 1914 in Lexington, Virginia. Living in the Shenandoah Valley, he developed a love of history at an early age, and went on to become a history master at the Kent School in Kent, Connecticut.

In 1942 Mr. Armstrong married Martha Stonecrest Williams. They had three children: Chrostopher, David and Mary.

Among William Armstrong's most noted works are *Study is Hard Work* (1956), *Through Troubled Waters* (1957), *87 Ways to Help Your Child in School* (1961), *Tools of Thinking* (1968), *Sounder* (1969), *Barefoot in the Grass: the Story of Grandma Moses* (1970), *Sour Land* (1971), *My Animals* (1972), and *Hadassah: Esther, the Orphan Queen* (1972).

INTRODUCTION

This unit has been designed to develop students' reading, writing, thinking, and language skills through exercises and activities related to *Sounder* by William Armstrong. It includes eighteen lessons, supported by extra resource materials.

The **introductory lesson** introduces students to one main theme of the novel through a bulletin board activity. Following the introductory activity, students are given a transition to explain how the activity relates to the book they are about to read. Following the transition, students are given the materials they will be using during the unit. At the end of the lesson, students begin the pre-reading work for the first reading assignment.

The **reading assignments** are approximately thirty pages each; some are a little shorter while others are a little longer. Students have approximately 15 minutes of pre-reading work to do prior to each reading assignment. This pre-reading work involves reviewing the study questions for the assignment and doing some vocabulary work for 8 to 10 vocabulary words they will encounter in their reading.

The **study guide questions** are fact-based questions; students can find the answers to these questions right in the text. These questions come in two formats: short answer required or multiple choice-matching-true/false. The best use of these materials is probably to use the short answer version of the questions as study guides for students (since answers will be more complete), and to use the multiple choice version for occasional quizzes. It might be a good idea to make transparencies of your answer keys for the overhead projector.

The **vocabulary work** is intended to enrich students' vocabularies as well as to aid in the students' understanding of the book. Prior to each reading assignment, students will complete a two-part worksheet for approximately 8 to 10 vocabulary words in the upcoming reading assignment. Part I focuses on students' use of general knowledge and contextual clues by giving the sentence in which the word appears in the text. Students are then to write down what they think the words mean based on the words' usage. Part II nails down the definitions of the words by giving students dictionary definitions of the words and having students match the words to the correct definitions based on the words' contextual usage. Students should then have an understanding of the words when they meet them in the text.

After each reading assignment, students will go back and formulate answers for the study guide questions. Discussion of these questions serves as a **review** of the most important events and ideas presented in the reading assignments.

After students complete reading the work, a lesson is devoted to the **extra discussion questions/writing assignments**. These questions focus on interpretation, critical analysis and personal response, employing a variety of thinking skills and adding to the students' understanding of the novel.

There is a **vocabulary review** lesson which pulls together all of the fragmented vocabulary lists for the reading assignments and gives students a review of all of the words they have studied.

The **group activity** has students working in small groups to research and discuss topics related to the novel. The group activity is followed by a **reports and discussion** session in which the groups share their ideas about the topics with the entire class; thus, the entire class is exposed to information about all of the themes and the entire class can discuss each theme based on the nucleus of information brought forth by each of the groups.

There are three **writing assignments** in this unit, each with the purpose of informing, persuading, or having students express personal opinions. The first assignment is to inform: students write a short composition about their own pets. The second assignment is to persuade: students create a bad situation caused by a pet, take one side of the argument and persuade the other side to take the action they think is necessary. The third assignment is to express personal opinions: students express their own opinions and questions regarding one of the topics discussed through the group activity.

There is a **nonfiction reading assignment**. Students are required to read a piece of nonfiction related in some way to *Sounder*. After reading their nonfiction pieces, students will fill out a worksheet on which they answer questions regarding facts, interpretation, criticism, and personal opinions. The nonfiction assignment for *Sounder* is incorporated into the group project.

The **review lesson** pulls together all of the aspects of the unit. The teacher is given four or five choices of activities or games to use which all serve the same basic function of reviewing all of the information presented in the unit.

The **unit test** comes in two formats: all multiple choice-matching-true/false or with a mixture of matching, short answer, multiple choice, and composition. As a convenience, two different tests for each format have been included.

There are additional **support materials** included with this unit. The **resource** sections include suggestions for an in-class library, crossword and word search puzzles related to the novel, and extra vocabulary worksheets. There is a list of **bulletin board ideas** which gives the teacher suggestions for bulletin boards to go along with this unit. In addition, there is a list of **extra class activities** the teacher could choose from to enhance the unit or as a substitution for an exercise the teacher might feel is inappropriate for his/her class. **Answer keys** are located directly after the **reproducible student materials** throughout the unit. The student materials may be reproduced for use in the teacher's classroom without infringement of copyrights. No other portion of this unit may be reproduced without the written consent of Teacher's Pet Publications, Inc.

UNIT OBJECTIVES - *Sounder*

1. Through reading William Armstrong's *Sounder*, students will consider the question, "Is crime ever justified?"

2. Students will demonstrate their understanding of the text on four levels: factual, interpretive, critical and personal.

3. Students will discuss segregation, illiteracy, poverty, bigotry, the Civil Rights Movement, and other relevant topics.

4. Students will be given the opportunity to practice reading aloud and silently to improve their skills in each area.

5. Students will answer questions to demonstrate their knowledge and understanding of the main events and characters in *Sounder* as they relate to the author's theme development.

6. Students will enrich their vocabularies and improve their understanding of the novel through the vocabulary lessons prepared for use in conjunction with the novel.

7. The writing assignments in this unit are geared to several purposes:
    a. To have students demonstrate their abilities to inform, to persuade, or to express their own personal ideas
        Note: Students will demonstrate ability to write effectively to <u>inform</u> by developing and organizing facts to convey information. Students will demonstrate the ability to write effectively to <u>persuade</u> by selecting and organizing relevant information, establishing an argumentative purpose, and by designing an appropriate strategy for an identified audience. Students will demonstrate the ability to write effectively to <u>express personal ideas</u> by selecting a form and its appropriate elements.
    b. To check the students' reading comprehension
    c. To make students think about the ideas presented by the novel
    d. To encourage logical thinking
    e. To provide an opportunity to practice good grammar and improve students' use of the English language.

8. Students will read aloud, report, and participate in large and small group discussions to improve their public speaking and personal interaction skills.

READING ASSIGNMENT SHEET - *Sounder*

Date Assigned	Reading Assignment (Chapters)	Completion Date
	1	
	2-3	
	4	
	5-6	
	7	
	8	

UNIT OUTLINE - *Sounder*

1 Introduction PV 1 Writing Assignment #1	2 Read 1 PV 2-3	3 Study ?s 1 Read 2-3 PVR 4	4 Study ?s2-3 Writing Assignment #2	5 Study ?s 4 PVR 5-6
6 Study ?s 5-6 PVR 7	7 Study ?s7 PVR 8	8 Study ?s 8 Extra ?s	9 Discussion	10 Library
11 Reports & Discussion	12 Reports & Discussion	13 Vocabulary	14 Writing Assignment #3	15 Film
16 Film	17 Review	18 Test		

Key: P = Preview Study Questions   V = Vocabulary Work   R = Read

STUDY GUIDE QUESTIONS

SHORT ANSWER STUDY GUIDE QUESTIONS - *Sounder*

Chapter I
1. Identify Sounder.
2. How did the father get Sounder?
3. Why did the boy stop going to school?
4. What did the family eat when they did not have solid food?
5. What did the boy's mother do in the evening after the small children went to bed?
6. What was cooking on the stove when the boy woke up the next morning? Why was this so unusual?
7. What did the boy's mother always do when she was worried?
8. What did the boy want to learn to do?

Chapter II
1. What happened to the boy's father?
2. Why were the sheriff and his deputies able to get near the cabin without the family knowing they were there?
3. What did the deputy tell the boy to do with Sounder?
4. What happened to Sounder as the wagon left?
5. Where did Sounder go after he was shot?
6. What did the boy find in the road where Sounder was shot? What did he do with it?
7. For what did the boy wish?

Chapter III
1. What instructions did the boy's mother give him before she went to town?
2. Why was the boy afraid of the houses with curtains on the windows?
3. Why did the boy's mother go to town?
4. Why did the boy go under the cabin?

Chapter IV
1. Where did the boy's mother believe Sounder had gone?
2. Why had the boy's mother brought home the vanilla flavoring?
3. What did the mother do with the large cake?
4. What did the red-faced man at the jail do to the cake?
5. What did the boy's father tell the boy when he visited him at the jail?

Chapter V
1. What did the boy forget to ask his father when he visited him in jail?
2. How long was Sounder away?
3. Besides Sounder's injuries from the gunshot, what was different about him?
4. What happened when the boy's father finally went to court?

Sounder Short Answer Study Questions Page 2

Chapter VI
1. When they boy began searching for his father, how did he prefer to travel? Why?
2. What one wonderful thing did the boy feel his journey accomplished?
3. What Bible stories did the boy like best?

Chapter VII
1. How did the boy know his father was not among the convicts white-washing the rocks?
2. What did the boy find in the trash barrel?
3. Why did the boy go into the school yard?
4. Why was the boy impressed by the teacher's cabin?

Chapter VIII
1. What did the teacher want the boy to do?
2. Why did the boy's mother agree to the teacher's idea?
3. What happened that made Sounder bark again?
4. Why was the boy's father crippled?
5. What happened to the boy's father?
6. Why did the boy dig a grave for Sounder before he left to go back to school?

KEY: SHORT ANSWER STUDY GUIDE QUESTIONS - *Sounder*

Chapter I
1. Identify Sounder.
    Sounder is a coon dog.
2. How did the father get Sounder?
    Sounder was a stray dog that came to the father.
3. Why did the boy stop going to school?
    He had to walk the eight miles each way, and it was too far to walk in the cold winter weather.
4. What did the family eat when they did not have solid food?
    They ate corn mush.
5. What did the boy's mother do in the evening after the small children went to bed?
    She picked the kernels out of the walnuts to sell at the store.
6. What was cooking on the stove when the boy woke up the next morning? Why was this so unusual?
    Pork sausages and ham were cooking. They only had pork sausages for Christmas, and they had only cooked ham once before in their cabin.
7. What did the boy's mother always do when she was worried?
    She hummed when she was worried.
8. What did the boy want to learn to do?
    He wanted to learn how to read.

Chapter II
1. What happened to the boy's father?
    Three white men came to the cabin and arrested the father for stealing the pork and ham.
2. Why were the sheriff and his deputies able to get near the cabin without the family knowing they were there?
    Sounder was out in the field waiting to go hunting and did not bark to warn them.
3. What did the deputy tell the boy to do with Sounder?
    He told him to take Sounder and hold him so they could leave the cabin.
4. What happened to Sounder as the wagon left?
    He got away from the boy and ran after the wagon. The deputy took his shotgun and shot Sounder.
5. Where did Sounder go after he was shot?
    He crawled under the porch and went far back under the cabin.
6. What did the boy find in the road where Sounder was shot? What did he do with it?
    He found part of Sounder's ear in the road. He took it back to the cabin to put under his pillow. He had heard that if you put something under your pillow and make a wish, the wish will come true.
7. For what did the boy wish?
    He wished for Sounder to be alive.

Chapter III
1. What instructions did the boy's mother give him before she went to town?
    She told him to watch the fire, to not leave the small children alone, and to warm the children some mush for supper. She also told him not to look for Sounder.
2. Why was the boy afraid of the houses with curtains on the windows?
    He was sure eyes were hiding behind the curtains watching him.
3. Why did the boy's mother go to town?
    She went to return the ham bone and the pork sausages. She also wanted to sell the walnuts to buy sowbelly and potatoes.
4. Why did the boy go under the cabin?
    He was searching for Sounder's body so he could bury him.

Chapter IV
1. Where did the boy's mother believe Sounder had gone?
    She thought he had gone into the woods to draw out the poison with oak-leaf acid.
2. Why had the boy's mother brought home the vanilla flavoring?
    She was going to make a cake for Christmas.
3. What did the mother do with the large cake?
    She put it in the box she had brought from the store, and she gave it to the boy to take to his father in jail.
4. What did the red-faced man at the jail do to the cake?
    He broke the cake into four pieces and squeezed it between his fingers.
5. What did the boy's father tell the boy when he visited him at the jail?
    He told the boy not to come back to visit him anymore. The father would send word by the visiting preacher.

Chapter V
1. What did the boy forget to ask his father when he visited him in jail?
    He forgot to ask where Sounder had first come to him on the road when he was a pup.
2. How long was Sounder away?
    He was away for two months.
3. Besides Sounder's injuries from the gunshot, what was different about him?
    He would not bark.
4. What happened when the boy's father finally went to court?
    He was sentenced to hard labor.

Chapter VI
1. When they boy began searching for his father, how did he prefer to travel? Why?
    He liked to follow the railroad tracks instead of the road. The roads went through towns, and he wanted to avoid people.

2. What one wonderful thing did the boy feel his journey accomplished?
   He found magazines and newspapers people had thrown away, and he was able to use them to practice his reading.
3. What Bible stories did the boy like best?
   He always liked to hear about David and Joseph.

Chapter VII
1. How did the boy know his father was not among the convicts white-washing the rocks?
   None of the men had come to the boy's defense when the guard threw the piece of iron and cut the boy's hand.
2. What did the boy find in the trash barrel?
   He found a book.
3. Why did the boy go into the school yard?
   He wanted the children to pump water for him so he could wash his cut fingers.
4. Why was the boy impressed by the teacher's cabin?
   This cabin had two lamps, two stoves, and shelves filled with books.

Chapter VIII
1. What did the teacher want the boy to do?
   He wanted the boy to live with him and go to school. In exchange, the boy would do chores for the teacher.
2. Why did the boy's mother agree to the teacher's idea?
   She hoped that the teacher could write letters to find out about the father. She also believed it was a sign from God.
3. What happened that made Sounder bark again?
   Sounder's master finally came home.
4. Why was the boy's father crippled?
   He had been caught in a dynamite blast in the prison quarry and had been crushed under an avalanche of limestone.
5. What happened to the boy's father?
   He and Sounder went hunting in the woods, where the boy's father died.
6. Why did the boy dig a grave for Sounder before he left to go back to school?
   He knew that now that Sounder's master was dead, Sounder had lost the will to live and would be dying soon.

MULTIPLE CHOICE STUDY GUIDE/QUIZ QUESTIONS - *Sounder*

Chapter 1

1. Identify Sounder.
   - A. Sounder is a Labrador Retriever.
   - B. Sounder is a coon dog.
   - C. Sounder is a German Shepherd.
   - D. Sounder is a bulldog.

2. How did the father get Sounder?
   - A. He won Sounder in a poker game.
   - B. He stole him from a man he was working for.
   - C. He bought him from a family that was moving.
   - D. The dog was a stray that followed the father home.

3. Why did the boy stop going to school?
   - A. He didn't have any shoes, and the teacher would not let him attend in his bare feet.
   - B. His parents needed him to work and earn money to support the family.
   - C. He had to walk the eight miles each way, and it was too far to walk in the cold winter weather.
   - D. He had had a fight with a few of the other boys, and had been expelled.

4. What did the family eat when they did not have solid food?
   - A. They ate corn mush.
   - B. They ate mashed fruit peels.
   - C. They ate bread pudding.
   - D. They ate cheese curds.

5. What did the boy's mother do in the evening after the small children went to bed?
   - A. She sat by the fire and read the Bible.
   - B. She made cornhusk dolls for them to play with.
   - C. She wove cloth from the cotton they grew.
   - D. She picked the kernels out of the walnuts to sell at the store.

6. True or False: When the boy woke up the next morning, the usual meal of pigs' feet and grits was cooking.
   - A. True.
   - B. False.

7. What did the boy's mother always do when she was worried?
   - A. She hummed.
   - B. She scrubbed the floor.
   - C. She bit her fingernails.
   - D. She cried and yelled at the children.

Sounder-Multiple Choice Study Quiz Questions Page 2

8. What did the boy want to learn to do?
    A. He wanted to learn to shoot a gun.
    B. He wanted to learn to ride a horse.
    C. He wanted to learn how to read.
    D. He wanted to learn how to play the harmonica.

Sounder-Multiple Choice Study Quiz Questions Page 3

<u>Chapter 2</u>
9. What happened to the boy's father?
    A. He was tarred and feathered.
    B. He was arrested by three white men.
    C. He was beaten and left for dead.
    D. He was run out of town on a rail.

10. Why were the sheriff and his deputies able to get near the cabin without the family knowing they were there?
    A. Sounder was deaf, and didn't hear them coming.
    B. Sounder was asleep.
    C. Sounder was out in the field waiting to hunt and did not bark to warn them.
    D. They had given Sounder a large piece of meat. He was so busy eating that he ignored them when they go near the cabin.

11. What did the deputy tell the boy to do with Sounder?
    A. He told the boy to take Sounder and hold him so they could leave the cabin.
    B. He told the boy to shoot the dog.
    C. He told the boy to lock the dog in the barn until they had driven away.
    D. He told the boy to feed the dog as a distraction.

12. What happened to Sounder as the wagon left?
    A. He got run over.
    B. He jumped into the wagon and was taken away along with the father.
    C. He got so excited he bit the boy and one of the younger children.
    D. He ran after the wagon and the deputy shot him.

13. What did Sounder do next?
    A. He sat in the middle of the road and wailed.
    B. He lay down in front of the fire and whined.
    C. He crawled under the porch and went far back under the cabin.
    D. He ran off into the field.

14. True or False: The boy found part of Sounder's ear in the road. He took it back to the cabin to put under his pillow.
    A. True.
    B. False.

15. The boy made a wish. What was it?
    A. He wished for enough food for his family.
    B. He wished for his father to come back.
    C. He wished for Sounder to be alive.
    D. He wished for a new dog.

Sounder-Multiple Choice Study Quiz Questions Page 4

<u>Chapter 3</u>

16. The boy's mother gave him instructions before she went to town. Which of the following statements was not one of the instructions?
    A. Watch the fire.
    B. Don't leave the small children alone.
    C. Warm up some mush for supper.
    D. Look for Sounder.

17. Why was the boy afraid of the houses with curtains on the windows?
    A. He had once been beaten by an older boy who came from such a house, and he had never forgotten it.
    B. His mother had told him that the curtains hid mean white devils.
    C. He was sure there were eyes hiding behind the curtains watching him.
    D. He thought the curtains were ghosts.

18. True or False: The boy's mother went to town to return the hambone and the pork sausages. She also wanted to sell the walnuts to buy sowbelly and potatoes.
    A. True.
    B. False.

19. Why did the boy go under the house?
    A. He had made a secret hid-away for himself.
    B. He was hiding some food he had stolen.
    C. He wanted to sweep out any evil spirits that might be lurking there.
    D. He was searching for Sounder's body so he could bury him.

Sounder-Multiple Choice Study Quiz Questions Page 5

<u>Chapter 4</u>

20. Where did the boy's mother believe Sounder had gone?
    A. She thought he had followed the father.
    B. She thought he had gone into the woods to draw out the poison with oak-leaf.
    C. She thought he had gone to a cave in the mountains to die.
    D. She thought he had been picked up along the road by some white men and killed.

21. What did the boy's mother bring home to use in the cake she was going to make?
    A. She brought home some cinnamon.
    B. She brought home some white sugar.
    C. She brought home some vanilla flavoring.
    D. She brought home a bar of chocolate.

22. What did the mother do with the large cake?
    A. She put it in a box and gave it to the boy to take to his father in jail.
    B. She sold it and used the money to buy food for her children.
    C. She let the children have it.
    D. She gave it to the sheriff as a peace offering. She hoped it would help to make things go easier for her husband.

23. True or False: The cake was bad. The mother didn't realize that the milk was sour and the eggs were rotten. The people who ate the cake got very ill.
    A. True.
    B. False.

24. The boy visited his father at the jail. What did the father tell the boy?
    A. The father told the boy to send letters instead of coming in person.
    B. The father said not to come any more, that he would send news by way of the visiting preacher.
    C. The father asked that his wife and the other children visit him as well.
    D. The father said the boy should be home working, not wasting his time on socializing.

Sounder-Multiple Choice Study Quiz Questions Page 6

Chapter 5

25. What did the boy forget to ask his father when he visited him in jail?
    A. He forgot to ask how long the father would be in jail.
    B. He forgot to ask if the father needed anything.
    C. He forgot to ask where the father kept his money hidden.
    D. He forgot to ask where Sounder had first come to him on the road when he was a pup.

26. How long was Sounder away?
    A. He was away for three days.
    B. He was away for one year.
    C. He was away for two months.
    D. He was a away for twenty-nine days.

27. Besides Sounder's injuries from the gunshot, what was different about him?
    A. He had a twitch that made him turn his head sideways every few seconds.
    B. He would not bark.
    C. He slept more than he used to.
    D. He kept his tail between his legs all of the time.

28. What happened when the boy's father finally went to court?
    A. He was sentenced to one year in the state prison.
    B. He was fined and then released on the condition that he leave town.
    C. He was sentenced to be hanged.
    D. He was sentenced to hard labor.

Sounder-Multiple Choice Study Quiz Questions Page 7

<u>Chapter 6</u>

29. True or False: When the boy began searching for his father, he followed the road very closely. He reasoned that he would meet more people that way, and might be able to find out more information about his father.
    A. True.
    B. False.

30. What one wonderful thing did the boy feel his journey accomplished?
    A. He got a lot of exercise and became very strong. He was sure he would be able to work hard and support his family when he returned from his journey.
    B. He got to see a lot of the country, and increased his knowledge of the world.
    C. He enjoyed the solitude. He felt like he had become a real man.
    D. He found magazines and newspaper's people had discarded, and he was able to use them to practice his reading.

31. What Bible story did the boy like best?
    A. He liked to hear about Moses leading his people to the promised land.
    B. He liked to hear about David and Joseph.
    C. He liked to hear about the Battle of Jericho.
    D. He liked to hear about Esau and Jacob.

Sounder-Multiple Choice Study Quiz Questions Page 8

<u>Chapter 7</u>

32. True or False: The boy knew his father was not among the convicts white washing the rocks because none of the men had come to his defense when the guard threw the piece of iron and cut the boy's hand.
    A. True.
    B. False.

33. What did the boy find in the trash barrel?
    A. He found a ham bone with enough meat on it to make a good dinner.
    B. He found a pair of shoes that were just a little too big for him.
    C. He found a loaded gun.
    D. He found a book.

34. Why did the boy go into the school yard?
    A. He wanted to try to steal some paper and a pencil.
    B. He was going to beg for food.
    C. He wanted the children to pump water for him so he could wash his cut fingers.
    D. He was lonely and wanted to play for a while before he resumed his grown-up task.

35. How did the boy feel when he was in the teacher's cabin?
    A. He was angry and jealous that some people had such luxury while others had none.
    B. He was impressed.

Sounder-Multiple Choice Study Quiz Questions Page 9

Chapter 8

36. What did the teacher want the boy to do?
    A. He thought the boy should continue on his search for his father. He gave the boy some books to read along the way.
    B. He thought the boy should return home. He thought the boy was much to young to be on the road alone.
    C. He wanted the boy to live with him and go to school. In return, the boy would do chores for the teacher.
    D. He wanted to have a childless couple in the town adopt the boy and bring him up correctly.

37. What did the boy's mother think of the teacher's idea?
    A. She agreed. She thought it was a sign from God.
    B. She disagreed. She thought the teacher was a bad influence on the boy.
    C. She was suspicious.
    D. She was angry and saddened.

38. The boy's father returned home. What did Sounder do?
    A. He jumped around on his three good legs and wagged his tail.
    B. He growled, then crawled under the house and hid.
    C. He looked straight at his master with his good eye and the empty socket.
    D. He barked.

39. How was the boy's father when he came home?
    A. He was stronger than ever, although he was very bitter.
    B. He was very depressed.
    C. He was crippled. He had been caught in a dynamite blast and had been crushed under an avalanche of limestone.
    D. He was energetic, and elated with the joy of seeing his family and dog again.

40. What happened to the boy's father?
    A. Sounder accidentally bit him. He got sick and died.
    B. He and Sounder went hunting in the woods, where the father died.
    C. The Sheriff saw him, thought he had escaped from the labor camp and shot him.
    D. He went fishing, fell into the water, and wasn't able to get out. He drowned.

41. True or False: Before he left to go back to school, the boy shot Sounder, and buried him in the grave with his father.
    A. True.
    B. False.

ANSWER KEY - MULTIPLE CHOICE STUDY/QUIZ QUESTIONS
Sounder

CHAPTER 1	CHAPTER 2	CHAPTER 3	CHAPTER 4
1. B.	9. B	16. D	20. B
2. D	10. C	17. C	21. C
3. C	11. A	18. B	22. A
4. A	12. D	19. D	23. B
5. D	13. C		24. B
6. B	14. A		
7. A	15. C		
8. C			

CHAPTER 5	CHAPTER 6	CHAPTER 7	CHAPTER 8
25. D	29. B	32. A	36. C
26. C	30. D	33. A	37. A
27. B	31. B	34. C	38. D
28. D		35. B	39. C
			40. B
			41. B

PREREADING VOCABULARY WORKSHEETS

Sounder Vocabulary Chapter 1

Part I: Using Prior Knowledge and Contextual Clues
　　Below are the sentences in which the vocabulary words appear in the text. Read the sentence. Use any clues you can find in the sentence combined with your prior knowledge, and write what you think the underlined words mean in the space provided.

1. The father turned to the cabin door. It was ajar.

2. Two successive Octobers the boy had started, walking the eight miles morning and evening.

3. His master's calloused hand would rub the great neck...

4. The trail barks seemed to be spaced with the precision of a juggler.

5. ...the coon dog would try to surprise his quarry and catch him on the ground.

6. He...tucked the edge of the coverlet under his body to keep out the cold that seeped up through the straw ticking.

7. "Cabins built on post would just float like boats, porch and all," he assured himself in a whisper.

8. The father sharpened the butcher knife with the whetstone he used to whet his scythe...

Part II: Determining the Meaning　　Match the vocabulary words to their dictionary definitions.

_____ 1. ajar　　　　　　A. Hardened; toughened
_____ 2. successive　　　B. Prey; a hunted animal
_____ 3. calloused　　　　C. Made certain; guaranteed; made confident
_____ 4. precision　　　　D. Mattress or pillow cover made of strong cotton
_____ 5. quarry　　　　　E. Following in an uninterrupted order; consecutive
_____ 6. ticking　　　　　F. Sharpen
_____ 7. assured　　　　　G. Partially opened
_____ 8. whet　　　　　　H. Accuracy; exactness

Sounder Vocabulary Chapters 2-3

Part I: Using Prior Knowledge and Contextual Clues
    Below are the sentences in which the vocabulary words appear in the text. Read the sentence. Use any clues you can find in the sentence combined with your prior knowledge, and write what you think the underlined words mean in the space provided.

1.   ...the rattle of wheels and each distinct hoofbeat <u>punctuated</u> the winter quiet.

2.   Even in summer a speck on the horizon was a <u>curiosity</u>...

3.   The noise seemed to undo the fearful shock that had held the smaller children <u>ashen</u> and motionless.

_____

4.-5.   There was another yelp, this one <u>constrained</u> and <u>plaintive</u>.

6.   There was a large spot of <u>mingled</u> blood, hair, and naked flesh on one shoulder.

7.   His little brother would murmur and be <u>addled</u> in his sleep tonight.

8.   There just seemed to be nothing else to fill up the <u>vast</u> lostness of the moment.

9.   In the matted Scotch-broom tangle he <u>visualized</u> the great tan body as he carefully picked each step.

Sounder Vocabulary Chapters 2-3 Continued

Part II: Determining the Meaning - Match the correct definitions to the words.

____ 1. punctuated A. Mournful; melancholy
____ 2. curiosity B. Confined; restrained; held back
____ 3. ashen C. Interrupted periodically
____ 4. constrained D. Formed a mental image
____ 5. plaintive E. Confused
____ 6. mingled F. Pale
____ 7. addled G. Great in size; huge
____ 8. vast H. Mixed
____ 9. visualized I. Something that arouses interest

Sounder Vocabulary Chapter 4

Part I: Using Prior Knowledge and Contextual Clues
    Below are the sentences in which the vocabulary words appear in the text. Read the sentence. Use any clues you can find in the sentence combined with your prior knowledge, and write what you think the underlined words mean in the space provided.

1. He wasn't hit in his <u>vitals</u>, I reckon.

2. "Oak leaves has strong acid that toughens the skin, just like the oak bark that they use to tan leather in the <u>tannery</u>.

3. With his knees still sore from crawling under the cabin, he <u>hesitated</u> a long time before he knelt on the frozen earth.

4. "Whatever you do, child, act perkish and don't <u>grieve</u> your father."

5. Long hallways,...ran from the door into the <u>dim</u> center of the building.

6. The horse doctor had been trying to <u>vaccinate</u> the bull in the neck...

Part II: Determining the Meaning   Match the vocabulary words to their dictionary definitions.

    ____ 1. vitals   A. Distress; cause to be sorrowful
    ____ 2. tannery   B. Lacking brightness or clarity
    ____ 3. hesitated   C. To give a vaccine to produce an immunity to an infectious
                                         disease
    ____ 4. grieve   D. Establishment where hides are tanned
    ____ 5. dim   E. Paused in uncertainty
    ____ 6. vaccinate   F. Body organs necessary for life

Sounder Vocabulary Chapters 5-6

Part I: Using Prior Knowledge and Contextual Clues
    Below are the sentences in which the vocabulary words appear in the text. Read the sentence. Use any clues you can find in the sentence combined with your prior knowledge, and write what you think the underlined words mean in the space provided.

1.-2. Ain't no use to <u>fret</u> yourself. Eat your supper, you must be <u>famished</u>."

3.   He heard the <u>damper</u> squeak in the stovepipe as she adjusted it.

4.   <u>Uncertainty</u> made the day of waiting longer too.

Part II: Determining the Meaning   Match the vocabulary words to their dictionary definitions.

    ____ 1. fret   A. Worry
    ____ 2. famished   B. An adjustable plate in the flue for controlling the draft of a
                                  furnace or stove
    ____ 3. damper   C. Doubtfulness; not knowing for sure
    ____ 4. uncertainty D. Extremely hungry

Sounder Vocabulary Chapter 7

Part I: Using Prior Knowledge and Contextual Clues
    Below are the sentences in which the vocabulary words appear in the text. Read the sentence. Use any clues you can find in the sentence combined with your prior knowledge, and write what you think the underlined words mean in the space provided.

1.   She seemed to understand the compulsion that started him on each long, fruitless journey with new hope.

2.-3.   His arms swung in apelike gyrations of glee, and he held another piece of iron in one hand and his cap in the other.

4.   His laughter had burst the button from his tieless shirt collar, and a white strip outlined his gaunt neck.

5.   ...the boy had not run but stood still and defiant...

6.   No one jeered at him or noticed him because he had crossed the street and was walking close up against the hedge on the other side.

7.   Just when he reached the cistern a wild commotion of barking burst from under the floor of the school.

8.   ....burst from under the building in pursuit of a pig....

9.   The boy found himself surrounded by strange inquiring eyes.

Sounder Vocabulary Chapter 7 Continued

Part II: Determining the Meaning - Match the vocabulary words to their dictionary definitions.

_____ 1. compulsion   A. Taunted; mocked
_____ 2. gyrations   B. Thin and bony
_____ 3. glee   C. Movements
_____ 4. gaunt   D. Asking
_____ 5. defiant   E. A receptacle for holding water, especially rain water
_____ 6. jeered   F. An irresistible motivation to do something
_____ 7. cistern   G. Joy
_____ 8. pursuit   H. The act of chasing after something
_____ 9. inquiring   I. Boldly resisting

Sounder Vocabulary Chapter 8

Part I: Using Prior Knowledge and Contextual Clues
    Below are the sentences in which the vocabulary words appear in the text. Read the sentence. Use any clues you can find in the sentence combined with your prior knowledge, and write what you think the underlined words mean in the space provided.

1. He read the story of Joseph over and over and never <u>wearied</u> of it.

2. The heat and drought of dog days had <u>parched</u> the earth...

3. As the figure on the road drew near, it took shape and grew <u>indistinct</u> again in the wavering heat.

4. The mouth was <u>askew</u> too.

5. The woman in the still rocker said, "Lord, Lord," and sat <u>suffocated</u> in shock.

6. ... how doctors had pushed and pulled and <u>encased</u> the numb side of his body in a cast.

Part II: Determining the Meaning Match the vocabulary words to their dictionary definitions.

    ____ 1. wearied   A. Enclosed
    ____ 2. parched   B. Physically or emotionally tired
    ____ 3. indistinct   C. Unclear
    ____ 4. askew   D. Made dry
    ____ 5. suffocated   E. To one side
    ____ 6. encased   F. Stifled

ANSWER KEY - VOCABULARY
Sounder

Chapter 1
1. G
2. E
3. A
4. H
5. B
6. D
7. C
8. F

Chapters 2-3
1. C
2. I
3. F
4. B
5. A
6. H
7. E
8. G
9. D

Chapter 4
1. F
2. D
3. E
4. A
5. B
6. C

Chapters 5-6
1. A
2. D
3. B
4. C

Chapter 7
1. F
2. C
3. G
4. B
5. I
6. A
7. E
8. H
9. D

Chapter 8
1. B
2. D
3. C
4. E
5. F
6. A

DAILY LESSONS

LESSON ONE

Objectives
1. To introduce *Sounder* unit.
2. To distribute books and other related materials
3. To preview the study questions for chapter 1
4. To familiarize students with the vocabulary for chapter 1

NOTE: Prior to this lesson you need to have prepared a bulletin board with background paper and the title MAN'S BEST FRIEND or some other appropriate title. Tell each student to bring in a picture of his/her pet(s) along with Writing Assignment #1 completed. You will find Writing Assignment #1 following Lesson One in this unit package.

Also prior to this lesson you need to have invited a guest speaker from your local SPCA or animal shelter -- even a veterinarian who will donate a little time would be great. Have your speaker talk to students about pet care, training pets, and/or recent issues relating to pets.

Activity #1
Tell students to get out their pictures and writing assignments. Have each student post the picture of the pet along with the writing assignment (under the picture) on the board. Each student should take about fifteen seconds to post his/her picture and, while posting the picture, tell the class a little about his/her pet.

Activity #2
Introduce your guest speaker for his/her presentation. Allow some time for students to ask questions.

TRANSITION: Tell students that the story they are about to read is titled *Sounder* -- the name of the family's dog in the story.

Activity #3
Distribute the materials students will use in this unit. Explain in detail how students are to use these materials.

Study Guides Students should read the study guide questions for each reading assignment prior to beginning the reading assignment to get a feeling for what events and ideas are important in the section they are about to read. After reading the section, students will (as a class or individually) answer the questions to review the important events and ideas from that section of the book. Students should keep the study guides as study materials for the unit test.

<u>Vocabulary</u> Prior to reading a reading assignment, students will do vocabulary work related to the section of the book they are about to read. Following the completion of the reading of the book, there will be a vocabulary review of all the words used in the vocabulary assignments. Students should keep their vocabulary work as study materials for the unit test.

<u>Reading Assignment Sheet</u> You need to fill in the reading assignment sheet to let students know by when their reading has to be completed. You can either write the assignment sheet up on a side blackboard or bulletin board and leave it there for students to see each day, or you can "ditto" copies for each student to have. In either case, you should advise students to become very familiar with the reading assignments so they know what is expected of them.

<u>Extra Activities Center</u> The Unit Resource portion of this unit contains suggestions for an extra library of related books and articles in your classroom as well as crossword and word search puzzles. Make an extra activities center in your room where you will keep these materials for students to use. (Bring the books and articles in from the library and keep several copies of the puzzles on hand.) Explain to students that these materials are available for students to use when they finish reading assignments or other class work early.

<u>Nonfiction Assignment Sheet</u> Explain to students that they each are to read at least one non-fiction piece from the in-class library at some time during the unit. Students will fill out a nonfiction assignment sheet after completing the reading to help you evaluate their reading experiences and to help the students think about and evaluate their own reading experiences.

<u>Books</u> Each school has its own rules and regulations regarding student use of school books. Advise students of the procedures that are normal for your school.

<u>Activity #3</u>

Show students how to preview the study questions and do the vocabulary work for Chapter 1 of *Sounder*. If students do not finish this assignment during this class period, they should complete it prior to the next class meeting.

WRITING ASSIGNMENT #1 - *Sounder*

PROMPT

People and animals share our planet, and probably since the earliest ages, people have had pets. In the next couple of weeks you will be reading a book about a dog named Sounder. Actually, the book is about more than just the dog, but the dog is important enough to have the book titled after him.

Your assignment has two parts. First, you are to find and bring in a picture of your pet. If you don't have a pet, bring in a picture of something you would like to have as a pet. If you don't have and don't want a pet, don't bring in a picture.

The second part is to write a little composition telling about your pet (if you have one), why you would like to have a particular kind of pet (if you don't have a pet but would like one), or why you don't have and don't want a pet.

PREWRITING

What can you say about your pet? Start with something easy. What's the pet's name? What kind of an animal is it? What does your pet do? Do you have a short tale to tell about your pet? Do you like your pet? Why? There are literally dozens of questions you could answer to tell about your pet. Consider these and other questions you think of relating to your pet. Brainstorm a list of things you would like to tell and/or interesting facts about your pet.

The problem is that you aren't going to write a whole book about your pet. In fact, you are only going to write as much as will fit on a 5" X 7" index card. That means you will have to sort through your ideas and choose only those facts and stories that are most interesting and tell the most about your pet in the shortest way.

If you don't have a pet but would like one, on your card tell what pet you would like to have, what you would name it, and why you would like to have one.

If you don't have a pet and don't want one, on your card explain why you don't want a pet.

DRAFTING

At the top of the card, print your pet's name on the left-hand side. Print your name on the right-hand side.

Write your facts/stories on the lines on the front of the card. That's the only space you have, so choose your words carefully for the best results possible.

PROOOFREADING

When you finish the rough draft of your paper, ask a student who sits near you to read it. After reading your rough draft, he/she should tell you what he/she liked best about your work, which parts were difficult to understand, and ways in which your work could be improved. Reread your paper considering your critic's comments, and make the corrections you think are necessary.

Do a final proofreading of your paper double-checking your grammar, spelling, organization, and the clarity of your ideas.

NONFICTION ASSIGNMENT SHEET - *Sounder*
(To be completed after reading the required nonfiction articles)

Name _____ Date _____

Title of Nonfiction Read _____

Written By _____ Publication Date _____

I. Factual Summary: Write a short summary of the piece you read.

II. Vocabulary
    1. With which vocabulary words in the piece did you encounter some degree of difficulty?

    2. How did you resolve your lack of understanding with these words?

III. Interpretation: What was the main point the author wanted you to get from reading his work?

IV. Criticism
    1. With which points of the piece did you agree or find easy to accept? Why?

    2. With which points of the piece did you disagree or find difficult to believe? Why?

V. Personal Response: What do you think about this piece? <u>OR</u> How does this piece influence your ideas?

LESSON TWO

Objectives
    1. To read chapter 1
    2. To give students practice reading orally
    3. To evaluate students' oral reading

Activity

    Have students read chapter 1 of *Sounder* out loud in class. You probably know the best way to get readers with your class; pick students at random, ask for volunteers, or use whatever method works best for your group. If you have not yet completed an oral reading evaluation for your students this marking period, this would be a good opportunity to do so. A form is included with this unit for your convenience.

    If students do not complete reading chapter 1 in class, they should do so prior to your next class meeting. Students should also preview the study questions and do the prereading vocabulary worksheet for chapters 2-3 prior to the next class meeting.

LESSON THREE

Objectives
    1. To review the main events and ideas from chapter 1
    2. To read chapters 2-3
    2. To preview the study questions for chapter 4
    3. To familiarize students with the vocabulary in chapter 4

Activity #1

    Give students a few minutes to formulate answers for the study guide questions for chapter 1, and then discuss the answers to the questions in detail. Write the answers on the board or overhead transparency so students can have the correct answers for study purposes. Note: It is a good practice in public speaking and leadership skills for individual students to take charge of leading the discussions of the study questions. Perhaps a different student could go to the front of the class and lead the discussion each day that the study questions are discussed during this unit. Of course, the teacher should guide the discussion when appropriate and be sure to fill in any gaps the students leave.

Activity #2

    Have students read chapters 2-3 of *Sounder* orally in class. Continue the oral reading evaluations. If students do not complete this assignment in class, they should do so prior to your next class period. Also prior to your next class period, students should do the prereading work for chapter 4.

ORAL READING EVALUATION - *Sounder*

Name _____ Class _____ Date _____

SKILL	EXCELLENT	GOOD	AVERAGE	FAIR	POOR
Fluency	5	4	3	2	1
Clarity	5	4	3	2	1
Audibility	5	4	3	2	1
Pronunciation	5	4	3	2	1
_____	5	4	3	2	1
_____	5	4	3	2	1

Total _____ Grade _____

Comments:

LESSON FOUR

Objectives
    1. To review the main ideas and events from chapters 2-3
    2. To give students the opportunity to persuade
    3. To give the teacher the opportunity to evaluate students' writing skills

Activity #1

    Give students a few minutes to formulate answers for the study guide questions for chapters 2-3, and then discuss the answers to the questions in detail. Write the answers on the board or overhead transparency so students can have the correct answers for study purposes.

Activity #2

    Distribute Writing Assignment #2. Discuss the directions in detail and give students ample time to complete the assignment.

LESSON FIVE

Objectives
    1. To review the main ideas and events from chapter 4
    2. To preview the study questions and vocabulary for chapters 5-6
    3. To read chapters 5-6

Activity #1

    Give students a few minutes to formulate answers for the study guide questions for chapter 4, and then discuss the answers to the questions in detail. Write the answers on the board or overhead transparency so students can have the correct answers for study purposes.

Activity #2

    Have students read chapters 5-6 orally in class. If you have not yet completed the oral reading evaluations, do so in this class period if at all possible. If you have completed the evaluations, have students read to each other in pairs. One student should read while the other student listens and follows along in his/her book. If students do not finish this assignment in class, they should do so prior to your next class meeting.

WRITING ASSIGNMENT #2 - *Sounder*

PROMPT

Pets can be a lot of fun, but they can also be the cause of big trouble. They innocently (or maybe not so innocently!) somehow get their masters tangled up in difficult situations. Whether it's digging up the neighbor's flower bed, chasing the neighbor's cat, running away in the park, biting the postal carrier, or any of hundreds of other possible situations, people with pets have to be prepared for almost any situation.

Your assignment is to choose one situation your pet (or *a* pet) could cause, and then as one of the people involved in the scenario, persuade the other party of your point of view. For example, if your dog has just dug up your neighbor's prize-winning tomatoes, you need to convince your neighbor that your dog will never dig in his garden again. Perhaps you would rather be the irate neighbor and convince the dog owner that he/she should get rid of the dog. Choose any situation involving pets and their owners. Perhaps your own pet has caused a little trouble at some time, and you would like to use that story as your focus. . . .

PREWRITING

First, create the scenario. What has happened? Make a few notes about the situation the pet has caused. Then, decide which character you would like to be in the scenario. Now, consider the situation from that character's point of view. What are that person's main concerns? Jot them down. What action will that person have taken? Write it down. What arguments can that person make to persuade the other side to take the action he/she wants taken? Jot them down. Pick your three best arguments and place a star next to them.

DRAFTING

Write an introductory paragraph in which you explain what has happened to whom and how it happened. Write from your character's point of view. At the end of this introduction, tell what action you think should be taken.

In the body of your composition, write one paragraph for each of the arguments you wish to make to persuade the other party to take the action you want taken. Fill out your paragraphs with explanations and/or examples to make your point(s) clear.

Write a concluding paragraph in which you clearly express your wishes and intentions and bring your composition to a close.

PROOFREADING

When you finish the rough draft of your paper, ask a student who sits near you to read it. After reading your rough draft, he/she should tell you what he/she liked best about your work, which parts were difficult to understand, and ways in which your work could be improved. Reread your paper considering your critic's comments, and make the corrections you think are necessary.

Do a final proofreading of your paper double-checking your grammar, spelling, organization, and the clarity of your ideas.

LESSON SIX

Objectives
1. To review the main ideas of chapters 5-6
2. To preview the study questions and vocabulary for chapter 7
3. To read chapter 7

Activity #1
Ask students to get out their books and some paper (not their study guides). Tell students to write down ten questions (and answers) which cover the main events and ideas in chapters 5-6

Discuss the students questions and answers orally, making a list of the questions with brief responses on the board. Put a star next to the students' questions and answers that are essentially the same as the study guide questions. (Be sure that all the study guide questions are answered.)

Activity #2
Give students about ten minutes to preview the study questions and do the vocabulary work for chapter 7.

Activity #3
Tell students that they should read chapter 7 prior to your next class meeting. If they have time after completing Activity #2, they may use the remainder of this class period to begin their reading silently.

LESSON SEVEN

Objectives
1. To review the main ideas and events from chapter 7
2. To preview the study questions and vocabulary for chapter 8
3. To read chapter 8

Activity #1
   Give students a few minutes to formulate answers for the study guide questions for chapter 7 and then discuss the answers to the questions in detail. Write the answers on the board or overhead transparency so students can have the correct answers for study purposes.

Activity #2
   Tell students that prior to your next class period they should have previewed the study questions, done the vocabulary work, and read chapter 8. Give students the remainder of this class period to work on this assignment. Students should read silently.

LESSONS EIGHT AND NINE

Objectives
1. To review the main ideas and events from chapter 8
2. To discuss *Sounder* on interpretive and critical levels

Activity #1
   Take a few minutes at the beginning of the period to review the study questions for chapter 8.

Activity #2
   Choose the questions from the Extra Discussion Questions/Writing Assignments which seem most appropriate for your students. A class discussion of these questions is most effective if students have been given the opportunity to formulate answers to the questions prior to the discussion. To this end, you may either have all the students formulate answers to all the questions, divide your class into groups and assign one or more questions to each group, or you could assign one question to each student in your class. The option you choose will make a difference in the amount of class time needed for this activity.

Activity #3
   After students have had ample time to formulate answers to the questions, begin your class discussion of the questions and the ideas presented by the questions. Be sure students take notes during the discussion so they have information to study for the unit test.

LESSON TEN

Objective
To review all of the vocabulary work done in this unit

Activity
Choose one (or more) of the vocabulary review activities listed below and spend your class period as directed in the activity. Some of the materials for these review activities are located in the Extra Activities section in this unit.

VOCABULARY REVIEW ACTIVITIES

1. Divide your class into two teams and have an old-fashioned spelling or definition bee.

2. Give each of your students (or students in groups of two, three or four) a *Sounder* Vocabulary Word Search Puzzle. The person (group) to find all of the vocabulary words in the puzzle first wins.

3. Give students a *Sounder* Vocabulary Word Search Puzzle without the word list. The person or group to find the most vocabulary words in the puzzle wins.

4. Use a *Sounder* Vocabulary Crossword Puzzle. Put the puzzle onto a transparency on the overhead projector (so everyone can see it), and do the puzzle together as a class.

5. Give students a *Sounder* Vocabulary Matching Worksheet to do.

6. Divide your class into two teams. Use *Sounder* vocabulary words with their letters jumbled as a word list. Student 1 from Team A faces off against Student 1 from Team B. You write the first jumbled word on the board. The first student (1A or 1B) to unscramble the word wins the chance for his/her team to score points. If 1A wins the jumble, go to student 2A and give him/her a definition. He/she must give you the correct spelling of the vocabulary word which fits that definition. If he/she does, Team A scores a point, and you give student 3A a definition for which you expect a correctly spelled matching vocabulary word. Continue giving Team A definitions until some team member makes an incorrect response. An incorrect response sends the game back to the jumbled-word face off, this time with students 2A and 2B. Instead of repeating giving definitions to the first few students of each team, continue with the student after the one who gave the last incorrect response on the team. For example, if Team B wins the jumbled-word face-off, and student 5B gave the last incorrect answer for Team B, you would start this round of definition questions with student 6B, and so on. The team with the most points wins!

7. Have students write a story in which they correctly use as many vocabulary words as possible. Have students read their compositions orally! Post the most original compositions on your bulletin board!

EXTRA WRITING ASSIGNMENTS/DISCUSSION QUESTIONS - *Sounder*

Interpretation

1. What point of view does Mr. Armstrong use for *Sounder*? How does this contribute to our understanding of the themes in the story?
2. Write a list of the main events in *Sounder* in chronological order.
3. Is the story of *Sounder* believable? Why or why not?
4. What are the main settings throughout the story? What do they add to the story?
5. Are the characters in *Sounder* stereotypes? If so, why are stereotypes used? If not, explain how they merit individuality?
6. What are the main conflicts in the story, and how are they resolved?
7. Why was Sounder given that name?
8. What was the mother's reaction to: the food being stolen, Sounder's being shot, the father's being arrested and put into prison, the boy's searching for his father, and the father's death?
9. The author used many bleak and dreary images to describe the characters' environment. Compile a list of the words and phrases used to describe the cabin, the countryside, the jail, the towns, the boy's journeys, and the boy's family.

Critical

10. Characterize William Armstrong's style of writing. How does it contribute to the value of the novel?
11. Compare Sounder and his master.
12. Explain why the book is called *Sounder* instead of something else.
13. Why was being able to read and having books so important to the boy?
14. Why was the dog the only character in the story with a name?
15. What does, "Only the unwise think that what has changed is dead" mean?
16. How does the author use details to add depth to the story?
17. What kind of a man is the father? How do you know?
18. What is the significance of the inevitability of Sounder's death at the end of the story?
19. Why are the little children included in the story?
20. What is the significance of the red-faced man at the jail?

Critical/Personal Response

21. If this story were told in the first person narrative by the boy, how would the story and its effect have changed?
22. Who or what is the main character of the story? Justify your answer.
23. *Sounder* is a short novel. Could anything have been gained by including more scenes from the time before or after the events of the story? If so, what could have been added and for what purpose. If not, explain why not.
24. What is "dignity," and how did this family exemplify that characteristic?
25. Do you think the father received fair punishment for stealing the food? Why or why not?

Sounder Extra Discussion Questions Page 2

26. Could this story have taken place in any location other than the South? If so, where and how? If not, why not?
27. Was this family's poverty different from the kind of poverty many people endure today? If so, how? If not, why not?
28. Suppose the boy had found his father right away. How would that have changed the story?

Personal Response
29. Did you enjoy reading *Sounder*? Why or why not?
30. Have you read any other books in which a pet was an important character in the story? Tell about those stories. How was *Sounder* like those stories, and how was it different?
31. Would you like to have had Sounder as a pet? Why or why not?
32. Are criminal and immoral acts like stealing ever justified? And if they are justified, does that make them less criminal and less immoral?

LESSONS ELEVEN THROUGH THIRTEEN

Objectives
1. To have students read nonfiction related to the story
2. To help students better understand the ideas presented in *Sounder*
3. To give students practice using library resources
4. To have students assume the responsibilities required by working in a group

Activity #1

Take students to the library. Divide your class into seven groups. Assign each group one of the following topics:
1. Sharecroppers: Who were they? Do they still exist today? Why or why not?
2. Poverty prior to government assistance: What did it mean to be poor before public assistance programs existed?
3. Segregation: What was it's cause and effect? Does it still exist today? Why or why not?
4. Illiteracy: What is the cause of illiteracy and how can it be cured? Compare illiteracy today with illiteracy 75 years ago.
5. Bigotry: What is it? Compare bigotry today with bigotry 50 years ago.
6. Civil Rights Movement: What is it, and how much progress has it made since 1960?
7. Religion: What is the role of religion in our society? Specifically concentrate on religion in schools and the dilemma about religious holiday displays in public places.

Each student in the group should find at least two articles about the group's topic. Students should take the first class period to find and read their articles.

Activity #2

After reading the articles, members of each group should meet to discuss the information they have found. Each student should give an oral summary of his/her articles to the group. As a group, then, students should consider all the information from all the articles and compile a presentation about the topic they have been assigned.

Activity #3

Then, each group should report its information to the whole class. Use these oral reports as springboards for discussion about the topics

LESSON FOURTEEN

Objectives
    1. To give students the opportunity to practice expressing their own opinions in writing
    2. To give the teacher the opportunity to evaluate students' writing skills
    3. To follow- up on the nonfiction reading assignment, giving students the opportunity to express their own opinions about one of the topics discussed

Activity

    Distribute Writing Assignment #3. Discuss the directions in detail and give students ample time to complete the assignment.

    While students are working, call individuals to your desk or some other private area for writing conferences based on the first two writing assignments in this unit. An evaluation form is included to help you structure your conferences.

LESSONS FIFTEEN AND SIXTEEN

Objectives
    1. To exercise students' analytical abilities
    2. To show students one person's visualization of the book

Activity #1
    Show the video or film of *Sounder*.

Activity #2
    After students have seen the film, hold a class discussion comparing and contrasting the film and the book.

LESSON SEVENTEEN

Objective
    To review the main ideas presented in *Sounder*

Activity #1
    Choose one of the review games/activities included in this unit and spend your class period as outlined there. Some materials for these activities are located in the Extra Activities section of this unit.

Activity #2
    Remind students that the Unit Test will be in the next class meeting. Stress the review of the Study Guides and their class notes as a last minute, brush-up review for homework.

WRITING ASSIGNMENT #3 - *Sounder*

PROMPT

The short novel *Sounder* touches on many themes and topics, many of which you have read about or heard reports about. As you were reading or listening, you may have had some ideas or questions of your own about what you were reading or hearing. Maybe you were so intent on other people's opinions that you didn't stop to think about your own. Your assignment is to write a composition in which you give your own opinions about one of the topics or themes related to *Sounder*.

PREWRITING

First, you have to decide what topic you want to write about. Consider all the topics covered in the group reports and other topics touched on in class discussions. Is there one that particularly interests you or one about which you have strong opinions? If so, your choice is clear. If you don't have any definite opinions about any of the topics, you need to stop and consider each one carefully and try to find your own opinions. Then, write about the one you have the most clearly defined opinions.

What is your topic? Write it down. Under that, jot down notes telling what you have heard or learned about the topic. Then, make some notes about your opinions relating to that topic. Next to each of your opinions, try to list a reason why you have that opinion. What information do you have that will support your feelings? Have you seen or read something? Is it your set of personal values that make you have this opinion? Jot down anything you can think of that will help to justify your opinion.

DRAFTING

Write an introductory paragraph in which you introduce your topic and give your "bottom line" opinions about the topic.

In the body of your composition, write one paragraph for each of your opinions related to the topic. Fill out each paragraph with any information that will help to support, justify, or explain your opinion.

Write a concluding paragraph in which you give your final thoughts about the issue and bring your composition to a close.

PROMPT

When you finish the rough draft of your paper, ask a student who sits near you to read it. After reading your rough draft, he/she should tell you what he/she liked best about your work, which parts were difficult to understand, and ways in which your work could be improved. Reread your paper considering your critic's comments, and make the corrections you think are necessary.

PROOFREADING

Do a final proofreading of your paper double-checking your grammar, spelling, organization, and the clarity of your ideas.

WRITING EVALUATION FORM - *Sounder*

Name _____ Date _____

Writing Assignment # ___ for *Sounder*   Grade _____

Grammar: excellent   good   fair   poor

Spelling: excellent   good   fair   poor

Punctuation: excellent   good   fair   poor

Legibility: excellent   good   fair   poor

Strengths:

Weaknesses:

Comments/Suggestions:

REVIEW GAMES/ACTIVITIES - *Sounder*

1. Ask the class to make up a unit test for *Sounder*. The test should have 4 sections: matching, true/false, short answer, and essay. Students may use 1/2 period to make the test and then swap papers and use the other 1/2 class period to take a test a classmate has devised. (open book) You may want to use the unit test included in this unit or take questions from the students' unit tests to formulate your own test.

2. Take 1/2 period for students to make up true and false questions (including the answers). Collect the papers and divide the class into two teams. Draw a big tic-tac-toe board on the chalk board. Make one team X and one team O. Ask questions to each side, giving each student one turn. If the question is answered correctly, that students' team's letter (X or O) is placed in the box. If the answer is incorrect, no mark is placed in the box. The object is to get three marks in a row like tic-tac-toe. You may want to keep track of the number of games won for each team.

3. Take 1/2 period for students to make up questions (true/false and short answer). Collect the questions. Divide the class into two teams. You'll alternate asking questions to individual members of teams A & B (like in a spelling bee). The question keeps going from A to B until it is correctly answered, then a new question is asked. A correct answer does not allow the team to get another question. Correct answers are +2 points; incorrect answers are -1 point.

4. Have students pair up and quiz each other from their study guides and class notes.

5. Give students a *Sounder* crossword puzzle to complete.

6. Divide your class into two teams. Use *Sounder* crossword words with their letters jumbled as a word list. Student 1 from Team A faces off against Student 1 from Team B. You write the first jumbled word on the board. The first student (1A or 1B) to unscramble the word wins the chance for his/her team to score points. If 1A wins the jumble, go to student 2A and give him/her a clue. He/she must give you the correct word which matches that clue. If he/she does, Team A scores a point, and you give student 3A a clue for which you expect another correct response. Continue giving Team A clues until some team member makes an incorrect response. An incorrect response sends the game back to the jumbled-word face off, this time with students 2A and 2B. Instead of repeating giving clues to the first few students of each team, continue with the student after the one who gave the last incorrect response on the team. For example, if Team B wins the jumbled-word face-off, and student 5B gave the last incorrect answer for Team B, you would start this round of clue questions with student 6B, and so on. The team with the most points wins!

UNIT TESTS

SHORT ANSWER UNIT TEST 1 - *Sounder*

I. Short Answer

1. Identify Sounder.

2. Why did the boy stop going to school?

3. What two things did the boy most want to do?

4. What happened to the father?

5. What did the boy's mother do with the ham and sausage? Why?

6. What was the significance of the red-faced man at the jail?

Sounder Short Answer Unit Test 1 Page 2

7. Describe the father's character.

8. Describe the mother's character.

9. What does the boy learn through his experiences during the time of the book?

Sounder Short Answer Unit Test 1 Page 3

II. Composition
    List in complete sentence form at least five main ideas presented in *Sounder*.
    Which of these ideas was the most important? Write a paragraph explaining your choice.

Sounder Short Answer Unit Test 1 Page 4

III. Vocabulary

   Listen to the vocabulary words and write them down. Go back later and fill in the correct definition for each word.

1.

2.

3.

4.

5.

6.

7.

8.

9.

10.

KEY: SHORT ANSWER UNIT TEST #1 - *Sounder*

I. Short Answer

1. Identify Sounder.

    Sounder was a hunting dog, faithful to his master. When his master was taken away to jail, Sounder was shot and nearly killed by the sheriffs. Sounder was used as a parallel to the master in the story.

2. Why did the boy stop going to school?

    He stopped because it was too far for him to walk in the cold.

3. What two things did the boy most want to do?

    He wanted to learn to read and to find his father.

4. What happened to the father?

    He was arrested for stealing, sent to jail, and sentenced to hard labor. He was in an accident -- almost crushed to death by stone. After the accident he was sent home again.

5. What did the boy's mother do with the ham and sausage? Why?

    She returned them. The family was poor but proud.

6. What was the significance of the red-faced man at the jail?

    The red-faced man was shown as a stereotype of the prejudiced lawman who lorded his authority and had no respect for the black prisoners or their families. He was a part of the system that inflicted unjust punishment upon the blacks in the South.

7. Describe the father's character.

    The father is shown as a quiet man with dignity who cares deeply for his family. He is not portrayed as a desperate criminal; rather, as a man trying to provide for his family.

8. Describe the mother's character.

    She is also shown as a quiet person with dignity. She worries about her husband and children and does all she can to care for and help them all. She is a woman of strength and convictions, but she is also compassionate, practical, and caring.

9. What does the boy learn through his experiences during the time of the book?

    He seems to already understand the importance of education, of learning to read. He learns that the world can be cruel to a black man; there are people in the world who will always be ready and willing to be oppressive. He sees, too, however, that there are also some caring people in the world, represented by the teacher. He learns through the examples of his parents, the teacher and Sounder that life is about surviving, living, loyalty, dignity and dying. The boy leaves his childhood and recognizes that life is a complex thing.

II. Composition

List in complete sentence form at least five main ideas presented in *Sounder*. Which of these ideas was the most important? Write a paragraph explaining your choice.

III. Vocabulary - Choose ten of the vocabulary words to read orally for Part IV of the unit test:

SHORT ANSWER UNIT TEST 2 - *Sounder*

I. Short Answer

1. Describe the father's character.

2. Describe the mother's character.

3. List three main ideas presented in *Sounder*.

4. In what ways does Sounder's life parallel the father's life?

5. Who was the main character in *Sounder*? Justify your answer.

Sounder Short Answer Unit Test 2 Page 2

II. Composition
    What did the boy learn through his experiences in the story *Sounder*?

III. Vocabulary
    Listen to the vocabulary words and write them down. Go back later and fill in the correct definition for each word.

1.

2.

3.

4.

5.

6.

7.

8.

9.

10.

KEY: SHORT ANSWER UNIT TEST 2 *Sounder*

I. Short Answer

1. Describe the father's character.
   The father is shown as a quiet man with dignity who cares deeply for his family. He is not portrayed as a desperate criminal; rather, as a man trying to provide for his family.

2. Describe the mother's character.
   She is also shown as a quiet person with dignity. She worries about her husband and children and does all she can to care for and help them all. She is a woman of strength and convictions, but she is also compassionate, practical, and caring.

3. List three main ideas presented in *Sounder*.
   There are many different ideas presented in *Sounder*. A few are:
   a. The importance of literacy
   b. The oppression of the black race in the South
   c. The domination of loyalty and the will to live
   d. The importance of pride and compassion
   e. The degradation of oppression and poverty
   f. The inhumanity of prejudice and bigotry
   g. The idea that suffering and death are as much a part of life as rejoicing and birth
   f. The idea that childhood is a time of innocence and as one grows up one has to understand and adapt to the realities of the world

4. In what ways does Sounder's life parallel the father's life?
   Sounder and the father are both totally loyal and devoted, and this loyalty and devotion gives them the capacity to survive and live even against terrible odds.

5. Who was the main character in *Sounder*? Justify your answer.
   Most of the action centers around the boy. The boy witnesses his father's being hauled off to jail and the shooting of Sounder. The boy has to assume responsibilities. The boy goes on a quest to find his father. The boy finds the father dead under the tree. The boy digs Sounder's grave. Although the relationships between dog and master and family and father figure prominently into the theme(s) of the novel, this author chooses the boy as the central character of the novel, seeing the novel primarily as a "coming of age" story with the secondary motif being that of the oppression of the Afro-American community in the South during this period.
   One could also make a case for either Sounder or the father being the central character as well. The answer to this question is open to your interpretation of the story.

III. Composition
What does the boy learn through his experiences during the time of the book?

He seems to already understand the importance of education, of learning to read. He learns that the world can be cruel to a black man; there are people in the world who will always be ready and willing to be oppressive. He sees, too, however, that there are also some caring people in the world, represented by the teacher. He learns through the examples of his parents, the teacher and Sounder that life is about surviving, living, loyalty, dignity and dying. The boy leaves his childhood and recognizes that life is a complex thing.

ADVANCED SHORT ANSWER UNIT TEST - *Sounder*

I. Short Answer

1. Who or what is the main character of the story? Justify your answer.

2. Characterize the father's role in the story relating to the theme development.

3. What did the boy learn through his experiences?

4. Explain the parallel between Sounder and his master.

5. Explain the role of education in the story.

Sounder Advanced Short Answer Unit Test Page 2

6. Choose another title for the story. Defend/explain your choice.

7. What is the significance of the inevitability of Sounder's death at the end of the story?

8. Discuss pride and dignity as motivational forces in the story *Sounder*.

9. What was the point of having Sounder and his master both become severely physically disabled? (The author could have written the story without either being injured; why did he choose this way?)

10. What was the mother's role in the story?

Sounder Advanced Short Answer Unit Test Page 3

II. Composition

Did you see this book as primarily a story about a boy growing up or as a story about the oppression of Afro-Americans in the South? Explain your answer using examples from the story.

Sounder Advanced Short Answer Unit Test Page 4

IV. Vocabulary

    Listen to the vocabulary words and write them down. Go back later and write a composition in which you use all of the words. The composition must relate in some way to *Sounder*.

MULTIPLE CHOICE UNIT TEST 1 - *Sounder*

I. Multiple Choice

1. Identify Sounder
    a. He was a hunting dog whose master was taken away.
    b. He was a boy who went searching for his father.
    c. He was a man who had been sent to a hard labor camp for stealing food.
    d. None of the above

2. Why did the boy stop going to school?
    a. His father needed help on the farm.
    b. His parents did not see the need for learning to read and write.
    c. It was too far for him to walk in the cold.
    d. He needed to care for Sounder.

3. What two things did the boy most want to do?
    a. Get even with the men who took away his father and shot his dog and find his father
    b. Learn to read and find his father
    c. Go to school and move North
    d. Find his father and understand why people treated him so badly

4. What happened to the father?
    a. He died in a labor camp.
    b. He returned to the farm bitter and broken..
    c. He committed suicide.
    d. He was severely injured in an accident.

5. What did the boy's mother do with the ham and sausage?
    a. She cooked them. Her husband would be punished anyway; the children might as well have a good meal or two.
    b. She finished cooking them and took them to the sheriff, trying to get him to be more lenient towards her husband.
    c. She returned them.
    d. She cooked them and sent them to her husband in jail, but when he got them they had been mauled so badly he couldn't eat them.

Sounder Multiple Choice Unit Test 1 Page 2

6. What was the significance of the red-faced man at the jail.
    a. He was symbolic of the devil.
    b. He was stereotypical of the oppressive whites in authority.
    c. He totally demoralized and frightened the boy.
    d. He was a Native American who was also oppressed by the whites in authority, but he still showed no sympathy toward the boy.

7. Describe the father's character.
    a. He was a desperate, hardened criminal.
    b. He had a chip on his shoulder and instigated trouble.
    c. He was depressed and hopeless.
    d. He was a quiet man with dignity.

8. Describe the mother's character.
    a. She was a woman of strength and convictions, compassionate and caring.
    b. She was a dominating woman who ruled the roost.
    c. She was a feeble woman, unsure of herself and unable to cope with stressful situations.
    d. She had given up hope and just went through the motions of living.

9. Which was not a main idea presented in *Sounder*.
    a. The degradation of oppression and poverty
    b. The inevitability of one's fate; the idea of destiny
    c. The domination of loyalty and the will to live
    d. The idea that childhood is a time of innocence

10. In what ways does Sounder's life parallel his master's?
    a. Both are loyal and devoted.
    b. Both are injured.
    c. Both have an especially strong will to survive.
    d. All of the above

11. Who was the main character in *Sounder*?
    A. The dog was.
    B. The father was.
    C. The boy was.
    d. The mother was.

Sounder Multiple Choice Unit Test 1 Page 3

12. Which of these is <u>not</u> something the boy learned through his experiences in the story?
    a. Hard work guarantees success.
    b. The world is complicated and can be cruel.
    c. There are people in the world who will always be oppressive.
    d. Life is about surviving, living, loyalty, dignity and dying.

III. Composition
    What is the main point of *Sounder*? What are we supposed to gain by reading it?

Sounder Multiple Choice Unit Test 1 Page 4

IV. Vocabulary - Match the correct definitions to the words.

____ 1. UNCERTAINTY   A. Worry

____ 2. GAUNT   B. Paused in uncertainty

____ 3. COMPULSION   C. Following in uninterrupted order; consecutive

____ 4. VACCINATE   D. Movements

____ 5. FRET   E. Joy

____ 6. ASKEW   F. Extremely hungry

____ 7. JEERED   G. Enclosed

____ 8. SUCCESSIVE   H. Mixed

____ 9. VISUALIZED   I. Formed a mental image

____ 10. CISTERN   J. Sharpen

____ 11. GLEE   K. A receptacle for holding water, especially rain water

____ 12. PLAINTIVE   L. Thin and bony

____ 13. SUFFOCATED   M. To one side

____ 14. MINGLED   N. An irresistible motivation to do something

____ 15. WHET   O. Mournful; melancholy

____ 16. GYRATIONS   P. Doubtfulness; not knowing for sure

____ 17. HESITATED   Q. To give a vaccine to produce an immunity to an infectious disease

____ 18. ENCASED   R. Body organs necessary for life

____ 19. VITALS   S. Taunted; mocked

____ 20. FAMISHED   T. Stifled

MULTIPLE CHOICE UNIT TEST 2 - *Sounder*

I. Multiple Choice

1. Identify Sounder
    a. He was a boy who went searching for his father.
    b. He was a hunting dog whose master was taken away.
    c. He was a man who had been sent to a hard labor camp for stealing food.
    d. None of the above

2. Why did the boy stop going to school?
    a. He needed to care for Sounder.
    b. His parents did not see the need for learning to read and write.
    c. His father needed help on the farm.
    d. It was too far for him to walk in the cold.

3. What two things did the boy most want to do?
    a. Learn to read and find his father
    b. Get even with the men who took away his father and shot his dog and find his father
    c. Go to school and move North
    d. Find his father and understand why people treated him so badly

4. What happened to the father?
    a. He was severely injured in an accident.
    b. He returned to the farm bitter and broken.
    c. He committed suicide.
    d. He died in a labor camp.

5. What did the boy's mother do with the ham and sausage?
    a. She cooked them. Her husband would be punished anyway; the children might as well have a good meal or two.
    b. She returned them.
    c. She finished cooking them and took them to the sheriff, trying to get him to be more lenient towards her husband.
    d. She cooked them and sent them to her husband in jail, but when he got them they had been mauled so badly he couldn't eat them.

Sounder Multiple Choice Unit Test 2 Page 2

6. What was the significance of the red-faced man at the jail.
   a. He totally demoralized and frightened the boy.
   b. He was a Native American who was also oppressed by the whites in authority, but he still showed no sympathy toward the boy.
   c. He was symbolic of the devil.
   d. He was stereotypical of the oppressive whites in authority.

7. Describe the father's character.
   a. He was depressed and hopeless.
   b. He was a quiet man with dignity.
   c. He was a desperate, hardened criminal.
   d. He had a chip on his shoulder and instigated trouble.

8. Describe the mother's character.
   a. She had given up hope and just went through the motions of living.
   b. She was a dominating woman who ruled the roost.
   c. She was a feeble woman, unure of herself and unable to cope with stressful situations.
   d. She was a woman of strength and convictions, compassionate and caring.

9. Which was not a main idea presented in *Sounder*.
   a. The idea that childhood is a time of innocence
   b. The domination of loyalty and the will to live
   c. The inevitability of one's fate; the idea of destiny
   d. The degradation of oppression and poverty

10. In what ways does Sounder's life parallel his master's?
    a. Both are injured.
    b. Both are loyal and devoted.
    c. Both have an especially strong will to survive.
    d. All of the above

11. Who was the main character in *Sounder*?
    A. The boy was.
    B. The father was.
    C. The dog was.
    d. The mother was.

Sounder Multiple Choice Unit Test 2 Page 3

12. Which of these is not something the boy learned through his experiences in the story?
    a. There are people in the world who will always be oppressive.
    b. The world is complicated and can be cruel.
    c. Hard work guarantees success.
    d. Life is about surviving, living, loyalty, dignity and dying.

III. Composition

You are the boy five years after the end of the story. You have been away from home for some time, going to school and working. Write a letter to your mother expressing your feelings about what transpired during the time of this story.

Sounder Multiple Choice Unit Test 2 Page 4

IV. Vocabulary - Match the correct definitions to the words.

____ 1. TICKING   A. Confined; restrained; held back

____ 2. DAMPER   B. Prey; a hunted animal

____ 3. ASHEN   C. Pale

____ 4. PARCHED   D. An irresistible motivation to do something

____ 5. FRET   E. Lacking brightness or clarity

____ 6. DEFIANT   F. Made certain; guaranteed; making confident

____ 7. MINGLED   G. Doubtfulness; not knowing for sure

____ 8. GYRATIONS   H. Mattress or pillow cover made of strong cotton

____ 9. DIM   I. Worry

____ 10. JEERED   J. To give a vaccine to produce an immunity to an infectious disease

____ 11. VACCINATE   K. Boldly resisting

____ 12. ASKEW   L. Movements

____ 13. UNCERTAINTY   M. Thin and bony

____ 14. COMPULSION   N. Mixed

____ 15. GAUNT   O. Taunted; mocked

____ 16. CONSTRAINED   P. Made dry

____ 17. QUARRY   Q. Something that arouses interest

____ 18. ASSURED   R. Formed a mental image

____ 19. CURIOSITY   S. To one side

____ 20. VISUALIZED   T. An adjustable plate in the flue of a furnace or stove for controlling the draft

ANSWER SHEET
Multiple Choice Unit Tests
Sounder

I. Multiple Choice	IV. Vocabulary
1. ___	1. ___
2. ___	2. ___
3. ___	3. ___
4. ___	4. ___
5. ___	5. ___
6. ___	6. ___
7. ___	7. ___
8. ___	8. ___
9. ___	9. ___
10. ___	10. ___
11. ___	11. ___
12. ___	12. ___
	13. ___
	14. ___
	15. ___
	16. ___
	17. ___
	18. ___
	19. ___
	20. ___

ANSWER KEY - *Sounder*
Multiple Choice Unit Tests

Answers to Unit Test 1 are in the left column. Answers to Unit Test 2 are in the right column.

      I. Multiple Choice   III. Vocabulary
      1. A B   1. P H
      2. C D   2. L T
      3. B A   3. N C
      4. D A   4. Q P
      5. C B   5. A I
      6. B D   6. M K
      7. D B   7. S N
      8. A D   8. C L
      9. B C   9. I E
     10. D D   10. K O
     11. C A   11. E J
     12. A C   12. O S
                   13. T G
                   14. H D
                   15. J M
                   16. D A
                   17. B B
                   18. G F
                   19. R Q
                   20. F R

UNIT RESOURCE MATERIALS

BULLETIN BOARD IDEAS - *Sounder*

1. Save one corner of the board for the best of student's *Sounder* writing assignments.

2. Take one of the word search puzzles from the extra activities section and with a marker copy it over in a large size on the bulletin board. Write the clue words to find to one side. Invite students prior to and after class to find the words and circle them on the bulletin board.

3. Write several of the most significant quotations from the book onto the board on brightly colored paper.

4. Make a bulletin board listing the vocabulary words for this unit. As you complete sections of the novel and discuss the vocabulary for each section, write the definitions on the bulletin board. (If your board is one students face frequently, it will help them learn the words.)

5. Do a bulletin board about crime and punishment. Make a chart of common crimes and the maximum penalties for punishment. Post articles about criminals who haven't gotten away with murder, criminals who have been severely punished for their actions.

6. Make a bulletin board about literacy. Post articles about programs in your community geared to helping those who are illiterate. Contact your local library or City Hall for posters, pamphlets, etc. about literacy.

7. Make a bulletin board about things that are gone but are still remembered.

8. See Lesson One for the bulletin board introductory activity.

EXTRA ACTIVITIES

One of the difficulties in teaching a novel is that all students don't read at the same speed. One student who likes to read may take the book home and finish it in a day or two. Sometimes a few students finish the in-class assignments early. The problem, then, is finding suitable extra activities for students.

One thing that helps is to keep a little library in the classroom. For this unit on *Sounder*, you might check out from the school library other related books and articles about poverty, segregation, illiteracy, government assistance programs, crimes and punishment, farming, careers in law enforcement or education, reviews of the movie *Sounder* or articles of criticism about *Sounder*. A biography of William Armstrong would be interesting for some students to read. Other works by William Armstrong would also make good additions to your in-class library.

Other things you may keep on hand are puzzles. We have made some relating directly to *Sounder* for you. Feel free to duplicate them.

Some students may like to draw. You might devise a contest or allow some extra-credit grade for students who draw characters or scenes from *Sounder*. Note, too, that if the students do not want to keep their drawings you may pick up some extra bulletin board materials this way. If you have a contest and you supply the prize (a record album or something like that perhaps), you could, possibly, make the drawing itself a non-refundable entry fee.

The pages which follow contain games, puzzles and worksheets. The keys, when appropriate, immediately follow the puzzle or worksheet. There are two main groups of activities: one group for the unit; that is, generally relating to *Sounder* text, and another group of activities related strictly to *Sounder* vocabulary.

Directions for these games, puzzles and worksheets are self-explanatory. The object here is to provide you with extra materials you may use in any way you choose.

MORE ACTIVITIES - *Sounder*

1. Pick a chapter or scene and have the students act it out on a stage. (Perhaps you could assign various scenes to different groups of students so more than one scene could be acted and more students could participate.)

2. Have students make a shadowbox of the inside of the cabin, the outside of the cabin or some other place in the story that the student may wish to depict.

3. Use some of the related topics noted earlier in the unit as topics for guest speakers or research papers.

4. Have students design a book cover (front and back and inside flaps) for *Sounder*.

5. Have students design a bulletin board (ready to be put up; not just sketched) for *Sounder*.

6. Have the class collect clothing, food, and books to give to a local charity.

7. Have students compose a list of what they think every person's basic rights should be. Have them compare their lists to real life.

8. Have your class plan a program against crime and vandalism for your neighborhood or school.

9. Hold a class discussion about what it means to be a minority citizen in America today. What are the current issues facing minority Americans, and what can this generations of students do to help?

10. Discuss ways to keep from being "poor." What can students do to be sure that they will be able to provide for their families without resorting to crime or depending on the government?

WORD SEARCH - *Sounder*

All words in this list are associated with *Sounder* with an emphasis on the vocabulary words chosen for study in the text. The words are placed backwards, forward, diagonally, up and down. The included words are listed below.

```
B I B L E N R E K S A U S A G E S M N J Y D H S
F H B Y H N S W K S C B S P S K V U C E E Z F N
F F B M S X V C N A B P F A C S G B N M S N F Y
C H I L D R E N H X C L C I X T G R M T W O S R
F G B R N M E Z Z O A W N F O G U U S H F A Z D
L Q C C E T R P S C O L R H W O H D Y V M Z C V
X G W W L H B W P L P L S C J Q W T G T C X T W
T S G N T Q S R L O Z Y N J G B V R S R W Z S B
S V V P V N S I J G R Q R Z W T L I S Y B B C D
C R T M D L P R M V E C H T W M R G C P W C H N
Z R J C M Z Y F R N G L E Z N H M M L M D Z H R
R X I B J T N E P L Q C I R C B C B F H Q S Y W
L H P P L R H L T C H N R P A L L R C H E L D C
T Q S X P C H Q A Y H W R E D H Y N L N L W U B
M N Z B A L O D Z E A C X E H O S S I E D R V G
Y H U E A F E O G L T Z R T A C O Z B N T A P V
M O T H E R E D N U O S B O X L A W F A T H E R
M O D R A J K U Q D T W H Q P G O E I P S I A R
L F Z E A C T P D X O K C F A S Y N R U D M H M
R U I N R E T N A L G G W M Z R S Z M P H A N D
```

BARK	EARTH	MUSH	SHERIFF
BIBLE	FATHER	NICKS	SHOTGUN
BOX	HAM	PILLOWCASE	SOUNDER
CAKE	HAND	PORCH	SOWBELLY
CALF	HUMMED	PREACHER	STEAL
CHILDREN	HUNT	READ	TEACHER
CHRISTMAS	JOURNEY	REAL	TO
COONDOG	KERNEL	RED	TWO
CRIPPLED	LANTERN	RUIN	WALNUT
CURTAINS	LAW	SAUSAGES	WOODPILE
DIE	MAGAZINES	SCHOOL	
EAR	MOTHER	SHARECROPPERS	

KEY WORD SEARCH - *Sounder*

All words in this list are associated with *Sounder* with an emphasis on the vocabulary words chosen for study in the text. The words are placed backwards, forward, diagonally, up and down. The included words are listed below.

```
    B I B L E N R E K S A U S A G E S   N   Y D
    F       S   K           S K   U   E E
      F   S   C   A       F A C   G N M
    C H I L D R E N H   C L C I   T   R M T W O S
          R     E     O A W N   O   U U         A
          E     P   C O     H   O H       M
            H   P L   S J           T
            S   L O                     S
              I     R             I
    C       P       E C         R
      R         R     L E     H
        I         E       I R C           S Y
          P   H L       R P A           E L   C
    T       P C   A   H W R E D H       N L   U
      N   B A L O D   E A C   E H O S   I E D R
      H U E A   E O   L T   R   A C O Z B   T A
    M O T H E R E D N U O S B O X L A W F A T H E R
        O   R A   K U   D T       P G O E I   S I A R
            E A     T       O         A S   N R U D       M
    R U I N R E T N A L G G   M     S   M P H A N D
```

BARK	EARTH	MUSH	SHERIFF
BIBLE	FATHER	NICKS	SHOTGUN
BOX	HAM	PILLOWCASE	SOUNDER
CAKE	HAND	PORCH	SOWBELLY
CALF	HUMMED	PREACHER	STEAL
CHILDREN	HUNT	READ	TEACHER
CHRISTMAS	JOURNEY	REAL	TO
COONDOG	KERNEL	RED	TWO
CRIPPLED	LANTERN	RUIN	WALNUT
CURTAINS	LAW	SAUSAGES	WOODPILE
DIE	MAGAZINES	SCHOOL	
EAR	MOTHER	SHARECROPPERS	

CROSSWORD - *Sounder*

CROSSWORD CLUES - *Sounder*

ACROSS

2. The stolen kind of meat
6. Bottom part of the leg
7. Sounder was one of these
8. Away from; not together
11. Holiday season
13. What mother did when she worried
15. Opposite of closed
16. The boy found Sounder's
17. Stop living
19. What the family ate when they did not have meat
21. Place one goes to learn
22. The --- faced man at the jail
23. Nut meat
24. Faster than walk
25. Opposite of poor
26. The boy's hurt appendage
29. Lamp; usually has oil fuel
31. County law enforcer
33. Sounder was away for --- months
35. Mother baked one for father
36. To take something that isn't yours
38. Eyes watched from behind these
41. They put the cake in one
42. Item on Mother's shopping list
44. Negative reply
45. Upon his return, Sounder would not ---; he would only whine
48. People have two; dogs have four
49. Actual; true; not imagined
50. The dog's name
51. Look at closely
52. Pilfered; taken without authorization
53. Wal---; hazel---; pea—

DOWN

1. He was sent to a labor camp
2. Look for animals to shoot
3. The boy found these to read
4. A trip
5. She returned the stolen meat
7. What Sounder and father became
9. The father would send word with him
10. Also
12. Mother returned the pork ---
14. Belonging to me
16. Dirt; our planet
18. Sounder crawled under it
20. The red-faced man ---ed the cake
21. The family's occupation
27. Small cuts and gouges
28. This was washed every week
29. Police enforce it
30. Instructor
32. Extreme dislike
34. The mother picked these kernels
35. The boy's mother told him not to leave them alone
37. Look at with your eyes
39. Sounder was shot by one
40. The father went -- jail
41. Book with stories the boy liked
43. Farmers usually own a lot of it
46. The boy wanted to do this
47. Opposite of in

CROSSWORD ANSWER KEY - *Sounder*

MATCHING QUIZ/WORKSHEET 1 - *Sounder*

____ 1. HUMMED   A. Dirt; our planet

____ 2. BOX   B. What Sounder and father became

____ 3. PORCH   C. Mother returned the pork ---

____ 4. LANTERN   D. The stolen kind of meat

____ 5. CURTAINS   E. The boy found Sounder's

____ 6. EARTH   F. Look for animals to shoot

____ 7. SAUSAGES   G. The father went -- jail

____ 8. SHARECROPPERS H. What mother did when she worried

____ 9. HAND   I. The dog's name

____ 10. LAW   J. Sounder crawled under it

____ 11. BIBLE   K. Eyes watched from behind these

____ 12. DIE   L. Lamp; usually has oil fuel

____ 13. CRIPPLED   M. The father would send word with him

____ 14. EAR   N. Police enforce it

____ 15. SOUNDER   O. The family's occupation

____ 16. PREACHER   P. Book with stories the boy liked

____ 17. TO   Q. They put the cake in one

____ 18. RED   R. Stop living

____ 19. HUNT   S. The --- faced man at the jail

____ 20. HAM   T. The boy's hurt appendage

KEY: MATCHING QUIZ/WORKSHEET 1 - *Sounder*

__H__	1. HUMMED	A. Dirt; our planet
__Q__	2. BOX	B. What Sounder and father became
__J__	3. PORCH	C. Mother returned the pork ---
__L__	4. LANTERN	D. The stolen kind of meat
__K__	5. CURTAINS	E. The boy found Sounder's
__A__	6. EARTH	F. Look for animals to shoot
__C__	7. SAUSAGES	G. The father went -- jail
__O__	8. SHARECROPPERS	H. What mother did when she worried
__T__	9. HAND	I. The dog's name
__N__	10. LAW	J. Sounder crawled under it
__P__	11. BIBLE	K. Eyes watched from behind these
__R__	12. DIE	L. Lamp; usually has oil fuel
__B__	13. CRIPPLED	M. The father would send word with him
__E__	14. EAR	N. Police enforce it
__I__	15. SOUNDER	O. The family's occupation
__M__	16. PREACHER	P. Book with stories the boy liked
__G__	17. TO	Q. They put the cake in one
__S__	18. RED	R. Stop living
__F__	19. HUNT	S. The --- faced man at the jail
__D__	20. HAM	T. The boy's hurt appendage

MATCHING QUIZ/WORKSHEET 2 - *Sounder*

____ 1. NICKS   A. Item on Mother's shopping list

____ 2. SOUNDER   B. Instructor

____ 3. CALF   C. The stolen kind of meat

____ 4. MAGAZINES   D. Nut meat

____ 5. LAW   E. The boy wanted to do this

____ 6. SOWBELLY   F. Sounder was shot by one

____ 7. TEACHER   G. Where wood is kept

____ 8. WOODPILE   H. The boy's hurt appendage

____ 9. MUSH   I. Bottom part of the leg

____ 10. HAND   J. To take something that isn't yours

____ 11. KERNEL   K. Police enforce it

____ 12. EAR   L. Sounder was away for --- months

____ 13. RED   M. The dog's name

____ 14. TWO   N. What the family ate when they did not have meat

____ 15. STEAL   O. Small cuts and gouges

____ 16. MOTHER   P. The family's occupation

____ 17. HAM   Q. The boy found Sounder's

____ 18. SHARECROPPERS   R. The --- faced man at the jail

____ 19. SHOTGUN   S. The boy found these to read

____ 20. READ   T. She returned the stolen meat

KEY: MATCHING QUIZ/WORKSHEET 2 - *Sounder*

__O__	1. NICKS	A. Item on Mother's shopping list
__M__	2. SOUNDER	B. Instructor
__I__	3. CALF	C. The stolen kind of meat
__S__	4. MAGAZINES	D. Nut meat
__K__	5. LAW	E. The boy wanted to do this
__A__	6. SOWBELLY	F. Sounder was shot by one
__B__	7. TEACHER	G. Where wood is kept
__G__	8. WOODPILE	H. The boy's hurt appendage
__N__	9. MUSH	I. Bottom part of the leg
__H__	10. HAND	J. To take something that isn't yours
__D__	11. KERNEL	K. Police enforce it
__Q__	12. EAR	L. Sounder was away for --- months
__R__	13. RED	M. The dog's name
__L__	14. TWO	N. What the family ate when they did not have meat
__J__	15. STEAL	O. Small cuts and gouges
__T__	16. MOTHER	P. The family's occupation
__C__	17. HAM	Q. The boy found Sounder's
__P__	18. SHARECROPPERS	R. The --- faced man at the jail
__F__	19. SHOTGUN	S. The boy found these to read
__E__	20. READ	T. She returned the stolen meat

JUGGLE LETTER REVIEW GAME CLUE SHEET - *Sounder*

SCRAMBLED	WORD	CLUE
RAKB	BARK	Upon his return, Sounder would not ---; he would only whine
ELBIB	BIBLE	Book with stories the boy liked
XBO	BOX	They put the cake in one
KCEA	CAKE	Mother baked one for father
FALC	CALF	Bottom part of the leg
DNCLHEIR	CHILDREN	The boy's mother told him not to leave them alone
IMCSSRHAT	CHRISTMAS	Holiday season
GNODOCO	COONDOG	Sounder was one of these
PCLDEPRI	CRIPPLED	What Sounder and father became
STNCRUAI	CURTAINS	Eyes watched from behind these
EDI	DIE	Stop living
REA	EAR	The boy found Sounder's
RTHEA	EARTH	Dirt; our planet
EHRFTA	FATHER	He was sent to a labor camp
MHA	HAM	The stolen kind of meat
DHAN	HAND	The boy's hurt appendage
MDHEMU	HUMMED	What mother did when she worried
THUN	HUNT	Look for animals to shoot
NURJYOE	JOURNEY	A trip
LKRNEE	KERNEL	Nut meat
NLNTREA	LANTERN	Lamp; usually has oil fuel
WAL	LAW	Police enforce it
ZAMSEGNIA	MAGAZINES	The boy found these to read
HTMORE	MOTHER	She returned the stolen meat
SMUH	MUSH	What the family ate when they did not have meat
KSNIC	NICKS	Small cuts and gouges
CPIWLASLOE	PILLOWCASE	This was washed every week
CHROP	PORCH	Sounder crawled under it
REPERHAC	PREACHER	The father would send word with him
ARED	READ	The boy wanted to do this
ALER	REAL	Actual; true; not imagined
DER	RED	The --- faced man at the jail
UNIR	RUIN	The red-faced man ---ed the cake
UGSAAESS	SAUSAGES	Mother returned the pork ---
OHOSLC	SCHOOL	Place one goes to learn
HERSPEAROCRSP	SHARECROPPERS	The family's occupation
FEHRFIS	SHERIFF	County law enforcer

VOCABULARY RESOURCE MATERIALS

VOCABULARY WORD SEARCH - *Sounder*

All words in this list are associated with *Sounder* with an emphasis on the vocabulary words chosen for study in the text. The words are placed backwards, forward, diagonally, up and down. The included words are listed below.

```
Q W U R H F W R J Q J L R L C T B K D S F Y H D
Y T S N F L M J P E V R D J G J K Q V A F S V Q
N M P Y C A N C L A E E X Y P D K W A R M I G A
G R I E V E M Q U A R R Y E N C A S E D T P J L
J Y E J V I R I W U S C E S Z O K T D A U A E D
M L R V D I X T S H V H H D U E I E L N R C T R
G I I A I P T S A H E I E E W F L S C W T I Y W
C N N N T S A N G I E T S N D D F T L C K S E P
X A I G Q I S L I A N D W U D P U O N U P M A D
T N L K L U O E F A U T E A A A U I C D P N F V
S A N L C E I N C N L N Y T T L T R E A O M V N
Q H N T O I D R S C N P T E A S I N S I T M O Y
D J D N V U T P I F U S D C I T I Z S U V E T C
C E L P E Y S F N N Z S Z D I A I I E K I I D G
R S F X M R S E Z H G R N Z R S C S X D S T N Q
N M T I S Q Y W D X G I X T H E T V E O D Y J J
M B Z R A Q H D D C H H S J R W L E I H N G C L
V A C C I N A T E N Q N T P C N T R R T G S R B
C N Z K B T T V Y H O M Z H B H U G D N S T B T
F S G C X F L Q W C K N S K T C W Q V C X G V Q
```

ADDLED	DEFIANT	INQUIRING	TANNERY
AJAR	DIM	JEERED	TICKING
ASHEN	ENCASED	MINGLED	UNCERTAINTY
ASKEW	FAMISHED	PARCHED	VACCINATE
ASSURED	FRET	PLAINTIVE	VAST
CALLOUSED	GAUNT	PRECISION	VISUALIZED
CISTERN	GLEE	PUNCTUATED	VITALS
COMPULSION	GRIEVE	PURSUIT	WEARIED
CONSTRAINED	GYRATIONS	QUARRY	WHET
CURIOSITY	HESITATED	SUCCESSIVE	
DAMPER	INDISTINCT	SUFFOCATED	

KEY: VOCABULARY WORD SEARCH - *Sounder*

All words in this list are associated with *Sounder* with an emphasis on the vocabulary words chosen for study in the text. The words are placed backwards, forward, diagonally, up and down. The included words are listed below.

```
                U               J                       D
            N F             P E         D                   A F   V
              C A             A E E               W A R M   I     A
        G R I E V E M Q U A R R Y E N C A S E D T P J
          Y E   V I R I W U S C E S   O K T D A U A E
        M L R V D I   T S H V H H D U E I E L N R         R
          G I I A I   T S A H E I E E W F L S C     T I
        C N N N T S A N G I E T S N D D F T L C     S E
            A I G Q I S   I A N D   U D P U O N U     A D
        T   L K L U O E   A U T E A A A U I C D P N     V
            A   L C E I N C   L N Y T T L T R E A O M
                N   O I D R S C   P T E A S I N S I T     O Y
        D       N   U T   I   U   D C I T I Z S U   E T C
            E       E   S       N   S   D I A I I E   I I D
                F       R   E       G   N   R S C S   D S T
                  I       Y   D       I   T   E T     E O
                    A                     S   R       E I H
        V A C C I N A T E           N   P           R R
                        T               O               U     N
                          C                   C
```

ADDLED	DEFIANT	INQUIRING	TANNERY
AJAR	DIM	JEERED	TICKING
ASHEN	ENCASED	MINGLED	UNCERTAINTY
ASKEW	FAMISHED	PARCHED	VACCINATE
ASSURED	FRET	PLAINTIVE	VAST
CALLOUSED	GAUNT	PRECISION	VISUALIZED
CISTERN	GLEE	PUNCTUATED	VITALS
COMPULSION	GRIEVE	PURSUIT	WEARIED
CONSTRAINED	GYRATIONS	QUARRY	WHET
CURIOSITY	HESITATED	SUCCESSIVE	
DAMPER	INDISTINCT	SUFFOCATED	

VOCABULARY CROSSWORD - *Sounder*

VOCABULARY CROSSWORD CLUES - *Sounder*

ACROSS
1. Distress; cause to be sorrowful
3. Extremely hungry
10. Look for animals to shoot
12. Establishment where hides are tanned
13. A receptacle for holding water, especially rain water
14. Great in size; huge
17. Joy
19. Look
21. Pale
22. Dog hair
23. Confused
25. Lacking brightness or clarity
26. Sharpen
28. Indefinite article
29. Small cuts and gouges
30. She returned the stolen meat
31. Sounder was away for --- months
33. Upon his return, Sounder would not ---; he would only whine
34. The --- faced man at the jail
35. Paused in uncertainty
37. Sounder couldn't see out of one ---
39. Mother baked one for father
41. Chances
43. A man's title
45. Prey; a hunted animal
47. Bottom part of the leg
49. Hardened; toughened
53. What the family ate when they did not have meat
54. Unclear
55. Something that arouses interest
56. Mixed

DOWN
1. Thin and bony
2. Body organs necessary for life
3. Worry
4. Following in uninterrupted order; consecutive
5. Enclosed
6. Confined; restrained; held back
7. Coordinating conjunction
8. To one side
9. Boldly resisting
11. The father went -- jail
14. To give a vaccine to produce an immunity to an infectious disease
15. Stifled
16. Doubtfulness; not knowing for sure
18. Police enforce it
20. Holiday season
21. Partially opened
24. An adjustable plate in the flue of a furnace or stove for controlling the draft
26. Physically or emotionally tired
27. The boy found Sounder's
32. Taunted; mocked
34. The boy wanted to do this
36. Made certain; guaranteed; making confident
38. Opposite of 'me'
40. Dirt; our planet
42. The act of chasing after something
44. Mattress or pillow cover made of strong cotton
46. Sounder's bark was an --- that strangers were coming
48. The red-faced man ---ed the cake
50. The boy could smell the --- of meat cooking
51. Period of time lasting 24 hours
52. Stop living

VOCABULARY CROSSWORD ANSWER KEY - *Sounder*

VOCABULARY WORKSHEET 1 - *Sounder*

____ 1. Partially opened
    A. Askew   B. Ajar   C. Damper   D. Whet

____ 2. Interrupted periodically
    A. Suffocated   B. Famished   C. Punctuated   D. Grieve

____ 3. Something that arouses interest
    A. Assured   B. Gyrations   C. Cistern   D. Curiosity

____ 4. Doubtfulness; not knowing for sure
    A. Mingled   B. Cistern   C. Uncertainty   D. Wearied

____ 5. A receptacle for holding water, especially rain water
    A. Constrained   B. Indistinct   C. Cistern   D. Ticking

____ 6. Great in size; huge
    A. Whet   B. Vast   C. Dim   D. Ashen

____ 7. Pale
    A. Ashen   B. Encased   C. Vaccinate   D. Jeered

____ 8. To one side
    A. Askew   B. Visualized   C. Uncertainty   D. Constrained

____ 9. Asking
    A. Inquiring   B. Assured   C. Indistinct   D. Ticking

____ 10. Stifled
    A. Encased   B. Vast   C. Suffocated   D. Gyrations

____ 11. Following in uninterrupted order; consecutive
    A. Successive   B. Compulsion   C. Famished   D. Ticking

____ 12. Mournful; melancholy
    A. Famished   B. Plaintive   C. Whet   D. Wearied

____ 13. An irresistible motivation to do something
    A. Compulsion   B. Punctuated   C. Constrained   D. Vast

____ 14. Confined; restrained; held back
    A. Tannery   B. Assured   C. Constrained   D. Vaccinate

____ 15. Boldly resisting
    A. Quarry   B. Defiant   C. Pursuit   D. Famished

____ 16. Confused
    A. Addled   B. Gaunt   C. Pursuit   D. Hesitated

____ 17. Mixed
    A. Quarry   B. Mingled   C. Visualized   D. Indistinct

____ 18. Unclear
    A. Indistinct   B. Visualized   C. Wearied   D. Curiosity

____ 19. To give a vaccine to produce an immunity to an infectious disease
    A. Glee   B. Vaccinate   C. Constrained   D. Indistinct

____ 20. Extremely hungry
    A. Famished   B. Vast   C. Calloused   D. Encased

KEY: VOCABULARY WORKSHEET 1 - *Sounder*

__B__ 1. Partially opened
    A. Askew   B. Ajar   C. Damper   D. Whet

__C__ 2. Interrupted periodically
    A. Suffocated   B. Famished   C. Punctuated   D. Grieve

__D__ 3. Something that arouses interest
    A. Assured   B. Gyrations   C. Cistern   D. Curiosity

__C__ 4. Doubtfulness; not knowing for sure
    A. Mingled   B. Cistern   C. Uncertainty   D. Wearied

__C__ 5. A receptacle for holding water, especially rain water
    A. Constrained   B. Indistinct   C. Cistern   D. Ticking

__B__ 6. Great in size; huge
    A. Whet   B. Vast   C. Dim   D. Ashen

__A__ 7. Pale
    A. Ashen   B. Encased   C. Vaccinate   D. Jeered

__A__ 8. To one side
    A. Askew   B. Visualized   C. Uncertainty   D. Constrained

__A__ 9. Asking
    A. Inquiring   B. Assured   C. Indistinct   D. Ticking

__C__ 10. Stifled
    A. Encased   B. Vast   C. Suffocated   D. Gyrations

__A__ 11. Following in uninterrupted order; consecutive
    A. Successive   B. Compulsion   C. Famished   D. Ticking

__B__ 12. Mournful; melancholy
    A. Famished   B. Plaintive   C. Whet   D. Wearied

__A__ 13. An irresistible motivation to do something
    A. Compulsion   B. Punctuated   C. Constrained   D. Vast

__C__ 14. Confined; restrained; held back
    A. Tannery   B. Assured   C. Constrained   D. Vaccinate

__B__ 15. Boldly resisting
    A. Quarry   B. Defiant   C. Pursuit   D. Famished

__A__ 16. Confused
    A. Addled   B. Gaunt   C. Pursuit   D. Hesitated

__B__ 17. Mixed
    A. Quarry   B. Mingled   C. Visualized   D. Indistinct

__A__ 18. Unclear
    A. Indistinct   B. Visualized   C. Wearied   D. Curiosity

__B__ 19. To give a vaccine to produce an immunity to an infectious disease
    A. Glee   B. Vaccinate   C. Constrained   D. Indistinct

__A__ 20. Extremely hungry
    A. Famished   B. Vast   C. Calloused   D. Encased

VOCABULARY WORKSHEET 2 - *Sounder*

____ 1. PURSUIT   A. Formed a mental image

____ 2. WHET   B. Distress; cause to be sorrowful

____ 3. VAST   C. A receptacle for holding water, especially rain water

____ 4. DIM   D. Taunted; mocked

____ 5. GYRATIONS   E. Lacking brightness or clarity

____ 6. SUCCESSIVE   F. Something that arouses interest

____ 7. VACCINATE   G. Confused

____ 8. ADDLED   H. Mattress or pillow cover made of strong cotton

____ 9. TICKING   I. Thin and bony

____ 10. WEARIED   J. To give a vaccine to produce an immunity to an infectious disease

____ 11. JEERED   K. Great in size; huge

____ 12. FAMISHED   L. Following in uninterrupted order; consecutive

____ 13. VISUALIZED   M. Extremely hungry

____ 14. GAUNT   N. Accuracy; exactness

____ 15. PRECISION   O. Physically or emotionally tired

____ 16. CURIOSITY   P. Sharpen

____ 17. CISTERN   Q. Made certain; guaranteed; making confident

____ 18. ASSURED   R. The act of chasing after something

____ 19. GRIEVE   S. Movements

____ 20. UNCERTAINTY   T. Doubtfulness; not knowing for sure

KEY: VOCABULARY WORKSHEET 2 - *Sounder*

__R__ 1. PURSUIT   A. Formed a mental image

__P__ 2. WHET   B. Distress; cause to be sorrowful

__K__ 3. VAST   C. A receptacle for holding water, especially rain water

__E__ 4. DIM   D. Taunted; mocked

__S__ 5. GYRATIONS   E. Lacking brightness or clarity

__L__ 6. SUCCESSIVE   F. Something that arouses interest

__J__ 7. VACCINATE   G. Confused

__G__ 8. ADDLED   H. Mattress or pillow cover made of strong cotton

__H__ 9. TICKING   I. Thin and bony

__O__ 10. WEARIED   J. To give a vaccine to produce an immunity to an infectious disease

__D__ 11. JEERED   K. Great in size; huge

__M__ 12. FAMISHED   L. Following in uninterrupted order; consecutive

__A__ 13. VISUALIZED   M. Extremely hungry

__I__ 14. GAUNT   N. Accuracy; exactness

__N__ 15. PRECISION   O. Physically or emotionally tired

__F__ 16. CURIOSITY   P. Sharpen

__C__ 17. CISTERN   Q. Made certain; guaranteed; making confident

__Q__ 18. ASSURED   R. The act of chasing after something

__B__ 19. GRIEVE   S. Movements

__T__ 20. UNCERTAINTY   T. Doubtfulness; not knowing for sure

VOCABULARY JUGGLE LETTER REVIEW GAME CLUES - *Sounder*

SCRAMBLED	WORD	CLUE
DELADD	ADDLED	Confused
JRAA	AJAR	Partially opened
NHSAE	ASHEN	Pale
KSWAE	ASKEW	To one side
DUSASER	ASSURED	Made certain; guaranteed; making confident
LOSUDCAEL	CALLOUSED	Hardened; toughened
RENSCIT	CISTERN	A receptacle for holding water, especially rain water
UPCSNOOILM	COMPULSION	An irresistible motivation to do something
ACSRTINNOED	CONSTRAINED	Confined; restrained; held back
SOTRIUYCI	CURIOSITY	Something that arouses interest
PEMADR	DAMPER	An adjustable plate in the flue of a furnace or stove for controlling the draft
DTENFAI	DEFIANT	Boldly resisting
IDM	DIM	Lacking brightness or clarity
SANECDE	ENCASED	Enclosed
SMFDAIHE	FAMISHED	Extremely hungry
TRFE	FRET	Worry
UNAGT	GAUNT	Thin and bony
LEGE	GLEE	Joy
VIGREE	GRIEVE	Distress; cause to be sorrowful
TNYRGIAOS	GYRATIONS	Movements
IHSAETDTE	HESITATED	Paused in uncertainty
DTNTCIINSI	INDISTINCT	Unclear
QNIUIGIRN	INQUIRING	Asking
EEEJRD	JEERED	Taunted; mocked
GNIDLEM	MINGLED	Mixed
RPCEDHA	PARCHED	Made dry
VPLNATIEI	PLAINTIVE	Mournful; melancholy
CIPRINSOE	PRECISION	Accuracy; exactness
UTPNCUDTAE	PUNCTUATED	Interrupted periodically
RUIUSPT	PURSUIT	The act of chasing after something
YQRUAR	QUARRY	Prey; a hunted animal
CUSEVSCSEI	SUCCESSIVE	Following in uninterrupted order; consecutive
TFUSACODEF	SUFFOCATED	Stifled
NNYREAT	TANNERY	Establishment where hides are tanned
NIKCITG	TICKING	Mattress or pillow cover made of strong cotton
TNTYUNRCEIA	UNCERTAINTY	Doubtfulness; not knowing for sure
NCVECATAI	VACCINATE	To give a vaccine